saying goodbye to the girls

D0861972

Find Joy on Your Journey!

Kim Wagner

saying goodbye to the girls

A LIGHT LOOK AT THE DARK SIDE OF CANCER

KIM WAGNER

Kim Wagner Speaks
www.kimwagnerspeaks.com

Cover and interior design by Annette Wood.
www.annettewoodgraphics.com

Editor: Heidi Mann, Writing Specialist
www.FinalTouchProofreadingAndEditing.com

Cover Photo: Meg Spielman Peldo

Back Photo: Tana Shereck

Photo Credits:
Page 16, 182, 183: Meg Spielman Peldo
Page 15, 78, 232, 233: Kensie Wallner
Page 166: Tana Shereck

Ordering Information:
Quantity sales. Special discounts are available on quantity purchases by corporations, associations, and others.

Printed in the United States of America

First Printing, 2015

ISBN 978-0-9961817-0-9

This book is dedicated to two wonderful individuals.

To my pea-picking mother, Audrey—
who, though rarely articulated, claimed her baby girl
as her favorite. That baby girl would be me.

To my kindest friend, Dave—
who has loved me through the years
with and without the girls—you are the best.

why?

I'm just saying.

My "girls" were a big part in defining me as a woman. To write *Saying Goodbye to the Girls* has been in my heart and mind since the day I was told, "You have breast cancer."

I began my fiftieth year of life overweight and inactive, acutely aware—but denying—that change was needed. I had experienced a half-century of scattered minutes becoming days, folding into weeks, and often, with unknown significance, swiftly flying into years. Hadn't I been advised of this phenomenon? Crazy stuff, this life is.

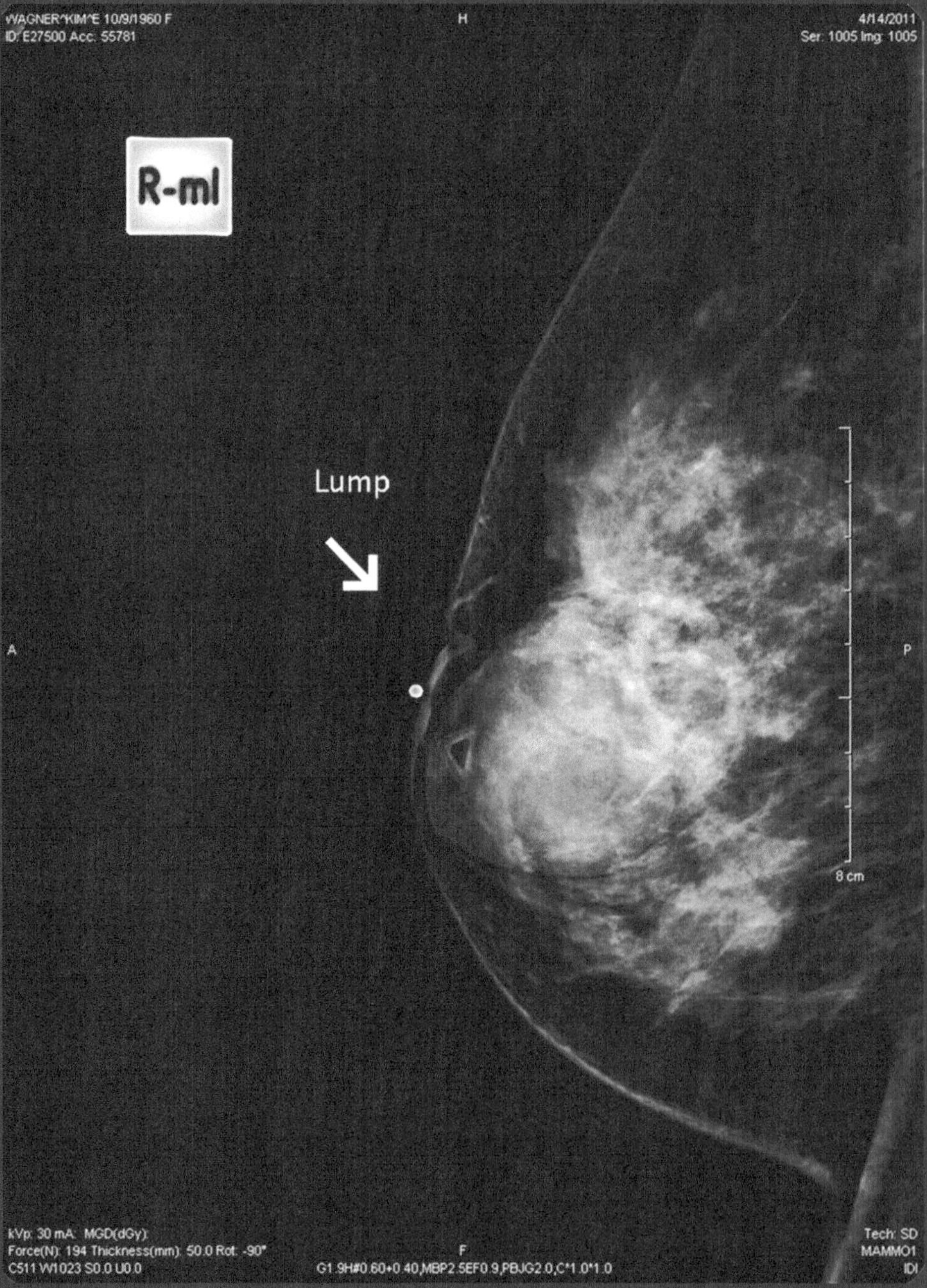
WAGNER^KIM^E 10/9/1960 F
ID: E27500 Acc. 55781
H
4/14/2011
Ser: 1005 Img: 1005
R-ml
Lump
A
P
8 cm
kVp: 30 mA: MGD(dGy):
Force(N): 194 Thickness(mm): 50.0 Rot: -90°
C511 W1023 S0.0 U0.0
F
G1.9H#0.60+0.40,MBP2.5EF0.9,PBJG2.0,C*1.0*1.0
Tech: SD
MAMMO1
IDI

I sat at the kitchen table in our home in Fargo, North Dakota. Around this very table, the ordained reverend and I had raised four outrageously above-average children. Four children, born within six years of each other, who, one by one, were pushed from our frenzied nest. The simplicity and complexity of everyday life was lived out at this table and, truth be told, we had done our job with heroic efforts.

Within my quiet house, I read and reread the surgical biopsy pathology report set before me:

Areas of significance:
Margin evaluation is problematic. Multiple areas showing tumor cells at the cauterized margins.
Tumor size: 5.5 cm.

Conclusion:
INVASIVE DUCTAL CARCINOMA

Lest I forget, and in the event there was any misunderstanding, the pathologist had underlined and highlighted "INVASIVE DUCTAL CARCINOMA."

Searching frantically in my sewing room for a tape measure, I contemplated my obvious lack of organizational wherewithal. Wishing my mother could stop over for a day to help organize my life's chaos, I could hear the wisdom in her voice: "Kim, have a place for everything and have everything in its place." My mother knew me so very well.

Locating the tape measure and flipping to its metric side, I studied the 5.5 line notation on the tape and overheard *"Jesus"* uttered from my lips. Let it be known, it wasn't a prayerful proclamation of my Savior's name.

This is my story, hopefully absent of weighted preaching. My goal is to share heartfelt snippets of my life, which has been profoundly impacted by breast cancer.

And the only thing people **regret** is that they didn't live **boldly** enough, that they didn't invest enough **heart**, didn't **love** enough. Nothing else really counts at **all**.

Ted Hughes

When diagnosed with breast cancer,
I wanted a way to share my thoughts
and feelings on this journey.
Journaling/blogging was the simplest
way to express myself while maintaining
contact with friends and family.

This is my story.

MY STORY

My mother, Audrey died of pancreatic cancer on January 25, 2009. Years earlier she went through two episodes of breast cancer. One resulted in a mastectomy and the other a lumpectomy.

I never heard her question, "Why me?" She was far from perfect, but her faith walk was impeccable. Jesus and Mom were best of friends—I envy that confidence. As she dealt with cancer, she was sure that her illness would mold her into a better, stronger, more compassionate, and loving individual. That it did.

However, as much as I am like my mother, we are dissimilar in a few ways. I do ask, "Why me?" Frequently, in fact.

And you know what? The answer is obviously simple—why not me? Life is not easy and seldom fair but this is my turn. I am humbled by your willingness to walk with me. Perhaps we can do this together.

June 13

My brother Lon called me a few nights back. He ended our conversation by saying, "I love you." I can't recall ever hearing him say he loved me. It was an unexpected sacred moment. See, if it takes me getting seriously sick to hear those lovely words, it just might be worth it.

I ask for patience and strength and a willing heart to accomplish that which needs to be done for today. Just today's stuff. Tomorrow is another day.

MY STORY

June 16

Still seems like I am stuck in a scary bad dream and may wake to discover I really don't have cancer. My life can be almost perfect again. Wouldn't that be something? After all, Dorothy woke up from her bad dream and decided that Oz wasn't so bad after all. Lesson to follow. Perhaps breast cancer is not so bad.

People ask how my kids are dealing with my cancer diagnosis (obviously this isn't a dream if so many people are asking the same question). To be honest, I have no idea.

All four kids have been great about calling and asking how things are going. But, it's hard to discern if they actually "get" that this illness might be very serious. They all end our conversations with, "I love you." Treasurable words to this 50-year-old mother's ears.

June 20

PET scan

1. Sit in fancy chair and get IV; have radioactive glucose injected into vein by triple-gloved RN

2. Sit in same chair for one hour with lights low and be advised, "Take a cat nap...don't let your mind wander...empty your head—just relax."

3. Move to room with doughnut-like shaped machine and lay on cold, hard, flat exam table while remaining PERFECTLY STILL for 40 minutes while doughnut machine detects/records energy given off by radio-tracer—converting to 3-dimensional computer pictures which are secretly shared by the staff...no patient peeking permitted

4. Go home and wait a few more days before visiting with surgeon who, hopefully is given access to view secret computer pictures (PET scan results) detecting if cancer has spread

the photography session

Change? Indeed. Cancer changed my life. But only for the better.

The clock noted 3:12 a.m. "I have breast cancer," I said out loud and briefly ruminated about the fact that in forty-eight hours, both breasts would be gone. Time was of the essence.

Although never approached about being photographed for a swimsuit calendar, I clearly had a fondness for my breasts. I had the sweet privilege of providing sustenance to four beautiful babies and, if encouraged with a good bottle of Malbec, I willingly shared them with my husband during lovemaking.

> God whispers to your **soul** and speaks to your **mind.** Sometimes, when you don't take the time to **listen,** he has to throw a brick at you. It's your **choice.** Listen for the whisper or wait for the brick.

I'm just saying.

I was fully cognizant that a surgical team would have my breasts tagged for pathology within two days—time was ticking! At 3:15 a.m., I determined that I needed to locate a professional photographer willing to preserve a visual of my fifty-year-old breasts.

A bit later— but still early—that morning, I called three photographers who, one by one, kindly declined my request. However, one suggested I contact Meg Spielman. He called her an "articulate, brilliant artist." I liked the sound of that, and it was all I needed to hear.

Meg did not flinch when I shared details as to what I wanted pictures taken of, and why. She was nothing short of the consummate professional. Spending several hours with me on June 30, 2011, Meg used her skillful lens and tender compassion to make me feel feminine, whole, and possibly borderline gorgeous.

She noted, "Kim, I want to see your joyful, playful side. Hey! You look worried, fearful, weary." *Really?*

"You are so brave," Meg hummed. "So, so brave." She clicked away.

In a three-hour procedure the following afternoon, I became breast-less. Goodbye, girls. In some obscure and terrifying way, losing my breasts felt a bit like losing good friends.

In April each year, South Africa has its annual National Cleavage Day (NCD). Begun in 2002, it was the brainchild of the Wonderbra brassiere marketer, working with various business entities based in Johannesburg. Marketing cleavage. There is, and will be forever, an allure about cleavage.

With all the emphasis in the United States on the display of breasts and cleavage, why is a day of such observance not organized here? Cosmopolitan, New Beauty, Glamour, and dozens of other "beauty" magazines are keenly aware that beautiful breasts on their covers, or images of the cleavage between the beautiful breasts, sell magazines—millions upon millions each month.

I've been asked, "Why would you want pictures taken of you in skimpy clothing?" My interpretation of this question: "Why would a Lutheran pastor's wife, who rightfully should be conservative, want to show off her overweight, curvy body in next to nothing?"

Why? Because there is more to me than being a conservative pastor's wife (Do note: *Who* is the conservative one in our family?) and I have never been timid about anything.

Why did I need BEFORE pictures taken? I wanted to remember my girls, soft and sensuous—nipples and all—before becoming a double amputee.

Elite Club

Carly Simon notes, "There's a feeling that if this had been a man's disease, it would have been licked already." There is some truth in this.

Besides Carly Simon, other famous breast cancer survivors include:

Jaclyn Smith,
Robin Roberts,
Joan Lunden,
Olivia Newton-John,
Suzanne Somers,
Melissa Etheridge,
Christina Applegate,
and Sheryl Crow.

Incidentally, the list is endless.

Being a breast cancer survivor puts me into an elite club. Obviously, I was in the wrong line at the right time because this is not an association that I ever intended to join. However, I am grateful to be a part of the club.

June 29

> The Lord will fight for you. You need
> only be still.
>
> Exodus 14:14

I admit that I have a hard time being still. My parents often scolded me for being wiggly—I've always wanted to be on the move. For 50 years I've been on the move—saying "yes" to many things that pulled me in all kinds of directions. Looking back, it is apparent that many of these commitments will not leave an impact on anyone or anything.

So God comes along and says, "My sweet little wiggly daughter, be still."

June 30

Marching orders...I am to be at the hospital by 7am tomorrow (Friday, July 1); surgery expected at noon. All is good. I feel strong and at peace; and very ready to have this over.

P.S. Please take care of Dave when I am unable.

obituaries

I read obituaries. Every day.

I scan for familiar faces, particularly of women who are my breast cancer sisters. I look for obvious wording that always gives me pause. Words such as: *courageously battled, died under hospice care, slipped into the arms of Jesus, passed peacefully surrounded by her loving family, called into glory*. The wording differs but the meaning is the same. They died.

I read about their lives, searching for commonality. Questions come to mind, and answers are rarely found.

My sister, who continues on, now that you are gone? Your spouse of five, fifteen, twenty-five, sixty years—how did he take your diagnosis? Did he encourage you to live every day to the fullest? Did he tenderly care for you when you could no longer care for yourself? Did you hit your bucket list hard, crossing off each item one by one? How many children do you claim, and where do they now live? Will family travel a long distance to come for the funeral? Did your children come home to participate in your dying process? Were songs sung, stories of childhood memories shared, and laughter heard? Did someone sit beside you and encourage you to get on the next train heading west? I want to picture it in my mind. I want to know. What does Jesus look like, and are there dogs where you are?

Who preceded you in death? Parents? Grandparents? Years back, were you in charge of walking about the display room at the local funeral home and choosing the casket your mother or father would be buried in? Were you responsible for selecting their clothing and jewelry? I hope so. Or will your

I want to know.

What does Jesus look like, and are there dogs where you are?

parents stand by your graveside or hold your eight pounds of cremated remains in an urn and ask, "Why couldn't it have been me?" Isn't it the correct order that children should bury their parents, not the other way around?

Do we have anything in common other than breast cancer? Did you perform in one-act plays or sing in the high school choir? Were you awarded the coveted Thespian of the Year trophy? Did you travel to European countries singing in a Christian ministry group? Did our paths cross? Were we college classmates? Did we ever work together, sing together, fundraise together, or sit in the same pew together at worship? Are we breast cancer friends? Did we ever have the opportunity to talk about living and dying?

Every day I read obituaries. Searching for my name.

Dave Wagner — July 1

Just a quick update, Kim underwent about three hours of surgery this afternoon. Doctor reported she came through the surgery well. He removed eleven lymph nodes under her right axillary area. They are being tested for cancer. Next Friday we are scheduled to meet with the doctor for a follow up exam and to go over the reports from pathology.

This has been a day we have appreciated the doctors and nurses at Sanford and what they have been able to do for Kim as well as for so many other people. Thanks for all your prayers and wonderful, positive thoughts. We are truly grateful for all of you.

By Dave Wagner — July 2

Kim arrived home from the hospital around 12:30 p.m. today. There were several people who questioned why Kim would want to return home so early when she could rest up at the hospital. She replied that there were five times during the night that the helicopter flew in and out (her room is two floors below the landing pad and as it landed, she reported that her entire room would shake). There were other sounds that kept her awake as well. Kim's belief is that if she wants to rest, the best place to be is at home. Kim's sister, Pat, is with us and we are grateful for her assistance.

July 3 (2 days post-surgery)

Many years ago Dave and I sang the song, WITH GRATEFUL HEARTS. Today, I am so grateful! For being home and able to sleep last night beside my sweet husband. For having a GOOD night of sleep (did not sleep well at the hospital) and for pain being manageable with outstanding meds. I am also so grateful for the beautiful new leather recliner that sweet Esther purchased just for me—it is so comfy and I can take great naps in the living room in it.

I am sleeping a lot. My brain is not functioning well—I blame that on loopy-happy drugs.

My chest and arms ache. Surprise.

July 5

Today has been a great day! Dave is an exceptional nurse—able to (with ease) empty Jackson Pratt drainage bottles and put clean gauze/tape over the tubing into my chest wall. Did I mention I am grateful?

I look forward to the day I can sit in a hot bubble bath with candles and a glass of wine. It will be a glorious day. My advice to you...

1. Sit in a bathtub with bubbles, candles and a glass of wine.

2. Sing all the songs you can remember at the top of your voice; make up lyrics if necessary.

3. Tell Jesus you are grateful for bubbles, candles and wine.

4. Get out of the tub and dry off. Call all your friends and tell them you love them and encourage them to take a long, hot bath.

the missing boobers

When storytelling, I often have to work hard to find the perfect anecdotal illustration for a story I want to share. This story took no searching.

As we know, children are frequently very candid. They just are what they are. Undisguised. I like that freshness about them. I wish more adults could be so uncomplicated and forthright. Perhaps we'd experience fewer misunderstandings.

Four weeks following a bilateral mastectomy, I reveled in the fact that I could finally get into tops that weren't button-down cotton. It reinforced that I was healing and felt like a major accomplishment.

> The **innocence** of children is what makes them stand out as a **shining** **example** to the rest of Mankind.
>
> Kurt Chambers

Of course, the tops needed to be plenty stretchy—but those with large openings and plenty of stretch did the trick!

I had made it through my first round of chemo, still had my own head of hair, and felt good enough to set off for the grocery store to pick up a couple items without anyone's assistance. I had selected a bright pink top and jean shorts for my outing.

I quickly picked up the five items I had gone for and headed to the check-out line. As a marketing strategy, of course, the selection of candy was conveniently located there, and without thinking twice, I quickly picked up a small bag of M&M's.

Ahead of me in line was a young mother with an attractive daughter, who I guessed to be four or five. The little gal had dark eyes and dark hair to match, cut in a darling bob. She was stunning, but rather shy. When almost to the check-out, the mother realized she had forgotten a jar of Miracle Whip. She instructed her young daughter to stay with the cart and noted, "I'll be back in just a minute, Maddie." I must have looked like a nice, trustworthy grandmother because she winked at me as she dashed to locate the missed item.

Suddenly I dropped my bag of M&M's. Bending over to retrieve them, I found myself eye to eye with Maddie. Her eyes grew very large and her little hand covered her mouth in a gesture of surprise. The words she uttered were priceless and straight-forward: "Lady, you lost your boobers."

I realized very quickly that by bending over, I had given this child a glimpse inside my gaping shirt at my scarred chest, booberless and all. "Yes, Sweetie, I had surgery."

"Oh, my!" Maddie gasped, and then recovered quickly. "Were they infected?" She said *infected* very distinctively—"in-FEC-ted."

I nodded. "Yes, one was badly infected," I said.

Instantly, she popped her left pointer finger into the air and whispered, "Was it *lopped* off? My dad got a bad in-FEC-tion in his finger and the doctor *lopped* it off." She gestured as one working the guillotine, ensuring that the finger indeed was cut clean off. She continued, "Did they *lop* your boobers off?"

Just then, Mother returned, embracing the jar of Miracle Whip and catching the tail end of our conversation. To say she was mortified would indubitably be an understatement. Her eyes met mine and in a quick, discerning glance to my chest, she surmised the situation, understanding fully.

She apologized adeptly. "Maddie can be precocious. I am so very sorry." Then she paused, looking at the candy in my hand. "Oh, please, allow us to purchase your M&Ms for you."

I smiled, shaking my head. "No need to apologize. I thoroughly enjoyed visiting with your daughter. I should be paying *you*. I couldn't make up speaking material this good."

If ever there is a tomorrow when we're not together... there is something you must always remember. You are braver than you believe, stronger than you seem, and smarter than you think. But the most important thing is, even if we're apart... I'll always be with you.

A.A. Milne, Winnie-the-Pooh

The young mother kept shaking her head in embarrassment, finally asking as they were about to depart with their grocery bags, "May I ask what your name is?"

"Kim—my name is Kim Wagner."

"Maddie, please apologize for being rude to Mrs. Wagner."

I could see the gears agitating in Maddie's little head. She spread her feet apart, and placed her hands on her hips before blurting, "I am so sorry they lopped your boobers off." The expression on her mother's face could not be replicated in a million years—it was sheer exasperation. I could do nothing but smile.

> And though she
> be but little
> she is fierce.
>
> William Shakespeare

They were leaving. The automatic doors had opened. Maddie's fingers were wrapped in her mother's hand. The sweetness of innocence was overwhelming, and I found myself wiping away a tear as it fell.

I was a privileged participant in this timeless moment. I hoped Maddie would not be scolded terribly for her honest comments. For she was very right . . . indeed, both of my boobers had been lopped off.

MY STORY

Dave Wagner — July 7

Every day Kim is feeling stronger. We met with the surgeon today and he is pleased with the progress of her healing. Due to tumor size and lymph node involvement, her cancer stage has been moved from a 2b and now is considered a 3b (for those of you who understand this). We are still very optimistic that Kim can conquer this.

As far as we can tell, our kids are doing well, though I think they'd all agree it would be nice to be closer to Fargo. Kim doesn't want people (especially the kids) to worry about us.

Kim's faith remains strong and both of us know that God is wrapping our family in his arms, frequently through doctors, friends, and prayers.

Sandy Hyland (God-mother and Cousin)
July 7

Sandy here. I spent a couple afternoons with Kim this week acting as her social secretary while Dave put in some time at work. On Tuesday I asked her before she went to lie down if there was anything I could do to help her and she said no, not unless I wanted to clean out her refrigerator and throw out all the gross stuff. I said she must have me mistaken with Pat who actually likes to do that sort of thing. Kim looked me up and down, all 5'2" of me, and said, "No, no, that would never happen!"

The following day I asked the same question and alas, this time she said she had a sewing project for me: I was to alter one of Dave's shirts into a sort of pajama top with pockets to hold her drain tubes. She had made a very nice one before going to the hospital, one that would easily sell for $40 at Healthcare Accessories, and needed another. So much for my quiet afternoon with Dr. Phil.

Dave took me downstairs to Kim's sewing room, an adventure in itself. (Ever seen "Hoarders"?) He was unable to get the overhead light to come on so rigged up another lamp for me, pointed out the on/off switch on the sewing machine and what he called "that thing" (the foot pedal), two things I might have been able to locate on my own. Then he was off. I pinned the first of the seven seams I needed to sew, and then spent a solid ten minutes trying to find the presser foot. I was absolutely laughing aloud down there all by myself. Then the overhead light flashed on, almost giving me a heart attack. I finally located the presser foot...and then realized I had no idea how to make the darned thing sew in reverse. I poked at a couple buttons (and I have no idea what I might have done to her settings) but nothing worked and I went back upstairs to wait for Sleeping Beauty to wake up and give me instructions.

Now you have to realize that at home I sew on a Coronado machine purchased at a hardware store in Crookston in 1960. Kim's machine is a Janome. I know because I saw the little logo.

I believe the Janome is the Cadillac of sewing machines while my antique is akin to a Model T.

Turned out that I had pressed one of the right buttons but didn't know I had to hold it in while it sewed backward for me. I finished the project and took it up to Kim, feeling the same trepidation I felt when I handed in my sad sewing projects to my home economics teacher back at Crookston High School. I think Kim gave me a B; Mrs. Johnson would not have been as kind. I told her she could wear it quickly while her nice top was in the wash and then change right back.

About that time Dave returned and I left for home. I think I was about halfway down the driveway when I heard them both break into peals of laughter.

It's great to hear Kim laugh, even at my expense! She's really doing so well, and your prayers and good wishes are part of that!

Bless you all for being in touch.
Good to hear from you!

July 11

Every life has its dark and joyful hours.
Happiness comes from choosing which
to remember.

Unknown

Today has not proven itself to be a dark day or for that matter, a particularly joyful day. Just an ordinary day. It's been ten days since surgery. I'm not "bouncing back" as I hoped (I'm the one who rode a horse the day after delivering a baby). However, each day I can see a bit of improvement.

I am determined to choose the joyful hours of each day to remember. And, right now I am thinking of each of you who take the time to read my blog entries. Thank you for being a part of my life. To quote Ben Folds, "I am the luckiest."

July 14

Exciting day—had another drain & tube re-moved this morning (if you've not had this done, you won't understand the exuberance of the hour). The last drain is still pulling 30 ml each day and my surgeon won't remove it until it is <20.

Lucas is home and he is a great help around here. He sat for a time and played piano yesterday. Lovely. To be able to comprehend Theoretical Physics and play Rachmaninoff's Prelude in C# Minor is astonishing—at least to me!

My sister Heidi, who is 11 months older than I am, is flying in tomorrow to spend the weekend in Fargo for our sibling reunion. I look so forward to her visit.

We see my Oncologist tomorrow. Hopefully there is a game plan all lined up for me. I am glad the surgery is over and my incisions are healing nicely.

kindly, no versed

I was scheduled for a surgical breast biopsy—a simple procedure, I was assured. From copious reading, I found that the suggested medicinal track for this type of procedure would be conscious sedation consisting of Midazolam (brand name Versed) given intravenously with local anesthesia injected at the incision site.

For some reason, the idea of conscious sedation did not sit well with me. I remembered a co-worker once telling me that upon the completion of her colonoscopy, she began to shriek at the top of her lungs, "Where is my husband's penis?" A logical question, I thought at the time. Isn't that what any woman would demand to know upon completion of such a procedure? She had experienced conscious sedation.

My fear was real. I pictured myself under the effect of Versed sharing intimate details about my sex life, the frequency at which I consume chocolate chips by the handful at 3 a.m., how many bowel movements I had each week, or a confession about my serious fabric addiction. What if someone I shared a pew with on Sunday mornings just happened to be the surgical tech in the operating room? After Versed was injected, my mouth would ramble and my pristine reputation would be ruined.

Be
yourself...
everyone
else is
already taken.

What's more, on the Mayo website I read that local anesthesia is a type of pain prevention used during minor procedures to numb a small site

46

where pain is likely to occur without changing the patient's awareness. For a biopsy, a numbing medication is injected into the area—sometimes several small injections—and after a few minutes the area should be completely numb. If the area still has sensation, additional injections or applications may be given to ensure total numbness.

Despite what the Mayo website said, a highly educated and trained doctor whacking into my breast with a scalpel was not what I considered a *minor* procedure. I could not imagine an injection (or two) of lidocaine adequately ensuring total numbness.

I had an episiotomy stitched up following the birth of my third child at Missouri Baptist Hospital in Saint Louis, Missouri. A handsome, young intern was assigned to stitch. Due to his lack of experience, he was not good at discreetly hiding the syringe prior to injecting. Real or not, I saw the needle he was about to insert into my bleeding flesh as at least three inches long. He said I would feel a bit of a sting. I'll admit that the sensation of that needle was nothing like that of pushing a

Godzilla-sized baby (7 lbs, 11 oz) out of my vaginal canal, but it did burn a tad. So, I insisted time and time again as he began to stitch, "I feel that."

"Really?" And the cute, young intern with sweet brown eyes would inject another shot of the wonder drug. My intention was to not feel any pain in my rear for a very long time. Being a quilter, I was quite sure this dashing intern did not know the best method of securing stitches. When I offered to give him a few tips, he said, "We're all done." After sharing such intimate moments, I found it rather odd how quickly he thanked me for being a good patient and then exited the room. His assignment completed, I never saw him again.

Again, I took note of information on the Mayo website: "General anesthesia is a treatment that renders you unconscious during medical procedures so you don't feel or remember anything that happens. General anesthesia is commonly produced by a combination of intravenous drugs and inhaled gasses (anesthetics).

> ## If you're
> # brave
> ### enough to say
> # goodbye,
> ### life will reward you with a new
> # hello.

"The 'sleep' you experience under general anesthesia is different from regular sleep. The anesthetized brain doesn't respond to pain signals or surgical manipulations.

"The practice of general anesthesia also includes controlling your breathing and monitoring your body's vital functions during your procedure. A specially trained physician, called an anesthesiologist, often in conjunction with a certified registered nurse anesthetist, administers general anesthesia."

Yes, I determined early on, it would be best to have general anesthesia administered for my *minor* procedure. I found comfort in knowing I would be rendered unconscious by a specially trained physician and a certified registered nurse anesthetist. There would be no penis talk coming from my lips.

July 16

Today we spoke with oncologist who reviewed the pathology report and discussed upcoming chemo treatment. If we get the okay from the surgeon, chemo will start next week. The plan is to undergo four initial treatments, one administered every two weeks and then followed up with twelve weekly treatments. He wants to hit it hard so that if there are any cancer cells in my body, they are destroyed. If all goes as planned, there will be sixteen treatments, followed by radiation.

July 18

I've been off of narcotics now for almost 48 hours. Still using Tylenol, but I am pleased to be off of codeine. Though it is good stuff.

This afternoon I received a call from the Roger Maris Infusion Center informing me of Thursday's schedule of events. Education at 8am followed by 3-4 hours of chemo.

Every day this becomes a bit more real and I can't deny that it is ME dealing with cancer. Even with the scars left from the bilateral mastectomy, this concept is hard to grasp. It's ME, folks. Not the bald woman in the checkout lane at the grocery store. It's ME.

MY STORY

July 19

Yeah! Folks, I am a free woman... no JP drains left in me. Dr. Bouton pulled the last this morning. Funny, I begged him to give me a shot of something to numb up the area prior to the "pull." Why? The last removal was a bitch—I'll leave it at that. But, he told me it would hurt more to inject Lidocaine than for him to simply pull. "Count to ten and it will be all over," he suggested.

DID YOU KNOW??? 12 plus inches are coiled up inside with a Jackson Pratt drain. I watched it come out and survived!

I am to be at the clinic/hospital tomorrow at 5 am to prepare for a 7 am porta cath insertion procedure. PLEASE tell me why they need 2 hours to put in an IV—perhaps this allows time for yoga/meditation exercises.

When you think about it, what other choice is there but to hope? We have two options, medically and emotionally: Give up, or fight like hell.
Lance Armstrong

Under conscious sedation, porta cath was inserted under my skin (upper left chest). Was told that I would remember nothing. They lied. I recall everything. I watched the clock—the whole procedure took less than 20 minutes. The assistants were discussing what edibles they were bringing to the staff potluck the following day. Important discussion, for sure. I've been told that the porta cath will make chemo administration much easier. Hope so. The sight hurts like heck tonight. Chemo starts tomorrow.

I got a fun fuchsia shirt from a friend at church. Printed in rhinestones on the front it reads:

CANCER chose the wrong DIVA

It's time for the diva to start fighting like hell.

the girls in the pea patch

When I was about fourteen years old, I was picking peas with my mom in our large garden on the farm. Sensing that my period was soon to start, I blurted, "My girls are so blasted sore today!"

My mother turned to me and said, "I didn't catch that. What girlfriends are mad at you?"

"Mother," I retorted, "I'm talking boobs—my *girls*," I said, pointing to the little mounds on my chest. "They hurt today." As was often the case in those years, my mother was so clueless. One would have thought that after raising six children, four being daughters, she would get in the *groove* and understand the "girls" lingo. I was her youngest child. Her baby. Her *favorite*, I reminded her frequently.

She shook her head as she kept putting peas at a feverish rate into the brown bag with LEEVER GROCERY printed on it. "Kim, you should call them what they are. They are not boobs or girls. They are breasts."

Oh, Mother, really?

> The
> **mother**
> **daughter**
> relationship
> is the
> most
> **complex.**
> Wynonna Judd

Mom saw this as a teaching opportunity. She began to tell me how special it was to be a woman. "God, in all His wisdom, made women very different from men," she expounded.

Really? Unbeknownst to my mother, I had come to comprehend the subtle differences in gender. I had witnessed by father whizzing behind his workshop on a few occasions and found it crazy-nuts how he could just pull his "thing" out of his pants and urinate. As a farm girl, I had perfected various methods of peeing in the bush, as well. From early failures I learned that it was best to actually squat to pee. I learned this after attempting to stand straight up, like my father did, telling myself to concentrate—surely I could make my urine stream in a fabulous arch *away* from my body just like Dad did—only to find the pee that exited my body running directly down my pant leg. Yes, women were different from men.

"God gave us, as women, the ability to carry a child inside of us." Now Mom had stopped picking pea pods and was really getting into this. She tenderly stroked her midsection. "How beautiful is that?" Perhaps her question was meant to be rhetorical; I felt it might be the appropriate time to remind her that I was her "favorite" child, but she could not be stopped.

Dear Mom,
I want some guppies. I know they are expensive but I can get them free from Dawn Eklund. If you let me have a tank of guppies, I will diligently feed and tend to them. And, I promise never to argue with you again. Even if you say no, I will love you always. But, I hope you say "yes."

Kim
(3rd grade)

"Honey, God gave us *breasts*"—seriously emphasizing the word, lest I misunderstand—"so we could fully embrace motherhood, allowing us the ability to provide the only source of nourishment needed for our baby, a baby created from a simple sperm and egg."

Holy smokes. Within me there arose trepidation that I might encounter another "sperm from father, egg from mother" story. I looked up into the cloudless blue sky and sparkling sun and asked Jesus for a quick, drenching rain shower. I pictured a mad dash to the house, the current discussion abating without further reflection.

"Kim," she continued, "last month I read in *Better Homes and Gardens* that breast milk is the ideal way to provide optimum nutrition for a newborn's delicate digestive system. That nutrition can only be found in breast milk (non-nursing moms, please don't take offense; this was in the early '70s), which is, incidentally, not found in *boobies*, but *breasts*." To make her point even more profound, she gently cupped her girls. "From now on, Honey, let's call them by their correct name."

My mother was a proud member of the 1945 graduating class at Miss Wood's Teachers Prep School in Minneapolis. She was the smart one in her family. There were times I had great admiration for her; other times (par for the course as a teenager), not so much. However, I had to hand it to her. That warm July day in a garden seven miles west of Crookston, Minnesota, Mom had accomplished an important conversation with her adolescent daughter en route to womanhood.

Mom got back to the business of serious pea-picking. I did as well, all the while wondering why *Better Homes and Gardens* would publish a story on breast milk. What was the correlation between breast milk and having a better home or garden?

Another day I would ask Mom, if breast milk was the perfect thing for a baby, why was I raised on formula? Her favorite little girl was never allowed to snuggle into her mamma's boobies for an afternoon snack. What gives?

All I knew for sure on that hot day in early July was that my girls were tender.

Dave Wagner — July 21

Kim finished her first chemo treatment today. She has fifteen more treatments to undergo. With this being her first one, she was a bit apprehensive. However, everything went well and her nurse, Tammy, did a superb job of explaining everything. Her sister, Pat, was also with us to lend support and to help pass the time. There were two chemo drugs given to her. The first was Doxorubicin (also known as Adriamycin). Then she received Cyclophosphamide (Cytoxan). She is resting now at home, saying she's a bit tired. Tomorrow she will go in to receive a shot of Neulasta to help stimulate the growth of white blood cells. At this time we do not know how Kim will react to the chemo therapy.

Thanks again for all your thoughts and prayers.

How will I grow from this experience? Will I be a better, more compassionate listener, a stronger motivational speaker—a willing, giving advocate for others walking their own cancer pilgrimage? How will I be of service to others? How will God's glory be seen in my story? Will I be strong enough?

facts, figures and fear

Over 1.5 million new cancer cases are anticipated each year. Over 1,500 people die of cancer every twenty-four hours across the United States. Each day, close to 4,200 people in the United States hear the words "You have cancer."*

Besides the news of a loved one's death, the words declaring a cancer diagnosis are perhaps the most dreaded words one anticipates. These were the words I heard on June 8, 2011, in a small recovery room at Essentia Hospital in Fargo, North Dakota. Dr. Tim Mahoney had just completed a surgical biopsy on my right breast. Dressed in blue scrubs, he entered quietly.

"Kim, we found cancer."

No fanfare. Just words. I wasn't surprised.

"I suspected so. Now what?"

"I had to make a larger incision than I would have liked." He paused briefly. "We'll be looking at a mastectomy in the weeks ahead. Further testing will be completed, and we'll take a look at the pathology report next week. I already spoke to your husband. Do you have any questions for me?"

My mind, still hazy from anesthesia (no Versed!), caused me to ponder briefly. Well, yes, I thought. I do have a couple questions: *Will I die from this? How much time do I have?* As if perfectly staged by a brilliant director, at that very instant my husband of nearly thirty years arrived at the door (stage right; I was a theatre major). A distraction. Dave's gentle blue eyes told me he knew. His wife had breast cancer.

Dr. Mahoney turned to Dave. "Do you have any questions for me?" From my recollection, neither of

> You never know how **strong** you are until being strong is the only **choice** you have.
>
> Bob Marley

us uttered much. "A nurse will be in shortly to remove your IV." He turned to go and then offered a quick addendum: "And you have a Jackson Pratt drain tube going home with you."

I always liked battle wounds! *Goodness, how cool is this?* I thought. *I get to take home a drain tube stuck in my side. Proof sufficient that I am a woman with a battle wound.*

The question *Will I die from this?* was not spoken out loud at that time. Nonetheless, the thought is provoking and has stuck in the recesses of my head to this day.

* 2010 Cancer Facts and Figures, American Cancer Society

July 26

The last few days have been marvelous! I've experienced one extraordinary gift followed by the next. To say I am grateful is an UNDERSTATEMENT!

1. Daughter, Margot sent me a cool hat from Goorin Bros., San Francisco

2. Sister, Pat maintained our household during my first chemo treatment

3. Friend, Denise wrote a wonderful, encouraging letter comparing the battle with cancer to that of her running (successfully) the marathon

4. Cards/letters on top of cards/letters (my basket is brimming) sharing love and concern

5. ICE CREAM from Pete and Mary

6. Bachelorette program shared with cousins, Susan and Sandy (WHO will Ashley choose between Ben and JP??)

7. A compassionate nurse, Tammy at the Roger Maris Infusion Center who spent hours with me last Thursday making my first chemo session a breeze (almost)

8. Friends, George and Pauline who sent me a bottle of the fabulous, Jo Malone's Grapefruit Cologne (which Oprah says takes five years off of one's age)

9. Friend, Mary who entertained our Yorkies, Wilson and Gimli last weekend, hauling them to the groomers and refusing to take payment for their darling hairdos

10. Lon and Nancy keeping my pup, Reggie (& he is such a pup yet) during his summer camp experience in WI

11. For Maggie and Amanda who snuck into our house & planted a "plush" stuffed cocker spaniel in the dog crate, joining an identical stuffed cocker spaniel that cousin Janet had sent earlier (you are nutty)

12. Food, food, food (& flowers, plants) from many ~ thank you!

The list could go on and on. The number of people who have asked, "What can I/we do?" - you are all precious!! I never figured that so many would be willing to assist us. I can hardly believe that almost 4,800 people are following my blog to date!

*If someone listens, or stretches out
a hand, or whispers a kind word
of encouragement, or attempts to
understand, extraordinary things begin
to happen.*

Loretta Girzartis

No, I would not wish anyone to go through breast cancer in my stead. However, noting what has transpired these past weeks and what lies ahead—I am grateful that God saw me fit to be a "carrier" so I could be a recipient of His unbelievable GRACE and MERCY. Believe it or not...I am learning to listen and to be still. Me, the wiggly one.

A Butterfly's Lesson

One day a small opening appeared in a cocoon; a man sat and watched for the butterfly for several hours as it struggled to force its body through the little hole. Then, it seemed to stop making any progress. It appeared as if it had gotten as far as it could and could not go any further.

So the man decided to help the butterfly. He took a pair of scissors and carefully opened the cocoon. The butterfly then emerged with ease. But, it had a withered body. It was tiny with shriveled wings.

The man continued to watch, expecting that at any moment, its wings would open, enlarge, expand; to be able to support the butterfly's body, and become firm.

Nothing happened! The butterfly spent the rest of its life crawling around with a withered body and shriveled wings. It never was able to fly.

What the man in his kindness and his goodwill did not understand was that the restricting cocoon and the struggle required for the butterfly to get through the tiny opening, was nature's way of forcing fluid from the body of the butterfly into its wings, so that it would be ready for flight once it achieved its freedom from the protective cocoon.

Sometimes struggles are exactly what we need in life.

If we were allowed to go through our life without any obstacles, it would cripple us. We would not be as strong as we could have been. And, we would never be able to fly.

author unknown

Prior to my diagnosis, perhaps I had become complacent and took far too much for granted. Whatever the case, I believe that down the road I will find that every struggle was for good reason and definitely worthwhile.

Eventful day. By the handfuls, my hair is falling out. Woke up to find hair all over my pillowcase. I certainly knew it was only a matter of time. But now that it's happening, it makes me melancholy. Truthfully, I've been feeling so good. Its difficult to believe that I am actually ill and will be bald in a matter of days, due to drugs trying to kill off the ugly cells (& other good cells the drugs just happen to run into along the way).

Last week, my friends, Mary and Theresa helped pick out my wig. It was actually quite a fun outing. They were great companions on my wig-picking trip and afterwards we went out for burgers and onion rings. All good.

Over the years, having attractive hair has been imperative to me (at times, too much so). After all, I was the Polk County Sugar Beet Queen and wore the crown proudly. Now my lovely locks will soon be gone. Oh my.

cherub choir

I love Jesus. Does He know?
Have I ever told Him so?
Jesus likes to hear me say
That I love Him every day.
Chorus (sung with gusto):
Yes, Jesus loves me! Yes, Jesus loves me!
Yes, Jesus loves me—the Bible tells me so.

Music has been crucial in helping me make it through this cancer journey. Music has long been a major part of my life, my faith, and my relationship with Dave. In fact, I don't think I would have considered marriage with anyone who could not sing. At college, Dave and I were paired up as madrigal singers—he, a tenor clad in a dress and tights. And yes, I fell in love with him as we strummed our guitars, moving from table to table, entertaining the guests.

My closest girlfriends sing, as well. It's in the friendship pact we have all signed. According to the third paragraph, "If you can't carry a tune, camaraderie with Kim Wagner is not in the cards." Though, sadly, I cannot dance. Learning to waltz, polka, and two-step is on my bucket list as skills I long to acquire before departing this life.

Though never an accomplished pianist, I have always loved music. There is something about a beautiful melody that can soothe my soul like nothing else. The old Lutheran hymns, imprinted on my heart, give me a sense of security that is difficult to fully comprehend.

Perhaps it all started back in Cora Louise's Cherub Choir at Trinity Lutheran Church in Crookston, Minnesota. Cora Louise directed this choir for what seemed like eighty-two years, maybe more. She was a lovely soul, but often chose songs of such difficulty that we sang with an obvious lack of confidence. Or with *humility,* one could say.

In my opinion, and that of several others, third-through sixth-graders are not capable of singing four-part harmony. At least not all together. The Cherub Choir consisted of approximately twenty young voices from five different family units: the Christiansons, the Zaffkes, the Windels, the Petersons and the Hansons.

As Cora Louise reminded us, "None of you has the ability to sing like an angel alone. But, put you all together, there is a glorious sound created, resounding on heaven's door . . . simply angelic." For many years I had great angst regarding death. If the glorious sound coming from the Cherub Choir sounded anything like the music heard on a regular basis in heaven, I had no desire to earn my wings.

Some of us were assigned to sing alto, some tenor, some bass, and a lucky few were called upon to be sopranos. I was always a bit envious of the sopranos because they could sing whatever they wanted. Some even found the melody line by accident. Even though my sister Heidi and I were both assigned to the alto section, we could not sit together. Our mother had told Cora Louise, one of her dearest friends—that her girls would start giggling something terrible if put side by side. So, Bobby Peterson was assigned to sit between us. Bobby didn't particularly like sitting between the Christianson sisters, nor did he like singing alto. So, when feeling contrary or whenever the spirit moved him, he sang bass. The only concern we had was that Bobby's voice was not bass. And, for that matter, what kid in third, fourth, fifth, or sixth grade has a voice low enough to sing bass? Certainly no one at Trinity Lutheran Church in Crookston, Minnesota.

So odd was his bass singing that Heidi and I would start giggling on either side of him. The sound he made was not for the faint of heart. It was a deep, troubling tone like that of a rabid squirrel's death howl. And the more we giggled, the louder Bobby sang—bass.

My Cancer Song

Tune: My Favorite Things
Words by Kim Wagner

Porta-cath and JP drains—Tylenol with codeine.
Lid-o-caine, Pril-o-kane and Pak-lit-tax-uhl
E-mend that's given to keep puke at bay
Just had my hair colored, Lord let it stay!

Cold sores, con-sti-pa-tion, Diarrhea and dry mouth
Sometimes the room spins, are we north or south?
People will comment that I'm looking swell
Insides are churning, but how can they tell?

Chemo brain, bone aches, Nights of not sleeping
Blood tests and PET scans, Weeks are a-creeping
Steroids that make me eat all that's in sight
How can I wonder when my clothes are tight?

Tax-o-tere, A-dro-my-cin, Cy-tox-an, the "red devil"
A shot of Neulasta to keep white cells level
Chemo-cocktails that make my head spin
Ben-e-dril, Ata-van—just make me grin!

Oncologist says, Radiologist agrees,
Treatments are doing the trick
Just when I think I have no more to give
The cancer is final--ly licked!

August 4

Your response to the seeming silence of God is to choose trust, based on what you know about his care. You know he shares your pain and takes the salt from our tears.

Randy Becton

Last night, about 3am, when I laid in the silence of the night trying to carry on a conversation with God—seriously, he was very silent. I said something like, "OK God, this is your daughter, (your favorite) Kim who lives in south Fargo and has breast cancer. Remember me?"

And I heard nothing. Nothing but the sound of the fan and Dave's breathing. Loud breathing, which sounded a lot like snoring (I'm just saying). Repeating myself, I spoke a bit louder, with a bit more urgency and tears trickling down my cheeks onto my pillow, "Where are you God?" I heard nothing.

"God, my hair is a mess, my heart is aching and chest is numb with ugly scars. Do you still love me like this?" Pausing, waiting for the lightning bolt, "Where are you God?"

About this time, Dave rolled over and gave me this sweet, tender embrace (still sleeping, I'm quite sure) and then rolled back, returning to slumber/snoring. I know it was God's arms around me. It was perfectly timed—as only He could master.

August 10

Yesterday afternoon I was fitted for my breast prostheses. Lovely flesh-tone silicone inserts which are placed into special prosthesis bras (equipped with pouches for the inserts). Pretty snazzy! Yes, for only $360 each... you too could add these to your collection of doodads. What is nuts—our insurance through the church does not cover the cost of bras. I don't get this. Believe me. Without the handy dandy over the shoulder boulder holder (thank you, Bette Midler for that clever visual), the prostheses would end up on the floor.

I'm feeling quite well. Just as I had been warned, this second round of chemo was a bit tougher than the first. More noticeable nausea and more hours of just feeling "punk" (as mother Audrey would say). Today I am finally feeling stronger; did not have to take multiple naps throughout the day. I do find I do better eating many small meals all day long—even a few bites of cottage cheese at 3 a.m. works great. The tummy cannot be empty & happy—crazy thing! Nausea is nasty stuff. OMG....what if I am actually pregnant? Think long and hard on that, will you...

August 18

Chemo consists of having all these powerful, very dangerous drugs pumped into my blood-stream and expecting they will do what they are supposed to do—without killing me.

God's delays are not God's denials.
Pastor James Cleveland

This is something I should pay attention to; perhaps all of us should take pause. Haven't we all found ourselves stranded and wondering how something good can come of a situation in our life that appears bleak? I feel stranded right now. Don't have the energy to accomplish a "hill of beans." The hill resembles a tall mountain.

Remember, if God puts a delay in our path, that doesn't mean that he won't be there to pick up the pieces and open new doors. To be honest, I believe that He intends to open doors wide for me with new opportunities presenting themselves. At the perfect time.

August 25

Life is good! I am doing my best to beat breast cancer. Last week I completed round three of chemo and only have 13 to go! Due to the steroids given during chemo, I am gaining weight. Actually, I'd be the perfect, chubby still model for a renaissance painting class, minus the soft, pendulous breasts (CLASS CHALLENGE—students would be required to improvise).

August 28

I hope to ...(not in order of significance)

1. Grow my hair back, perhaps curly this time around

2. See grandson, Leo graduate from kindergarten (or even high school!)

3. Celebrate 30 years of marriage (Nov. 28, 2011) and 40 years and 50 years...etc.

4. Participate in son, Isaac's wedding to Melissa (April 14, 2012)

5. See my sons, Lucas and Abram find a significant other to grow old together with

6. Tell many people about God's grace and mercy—reminding them that the mountain top and valley experiences add richness to the journey

'twas grace that taught my heart to sing

Ever since I was a little girl, I've always loved to sing. My earliest memory of publicly singing a solo is of standing in front of our large congregation at Trinity at the 11:00 a.m. service and singing the second verse of "Amazing Grace"—well, supposedly.

The morning of my solo, I stood in front of the large mirror in our bathroom, thinking that soon—very soon—I would have breasts. It was my ardent prayer. I really *needed* breasts to prove I was no longer a little girl. I asked my mother if I could soon have a bra of my own. Her reply was simply, "Oh, silly Kim."

But back to the solo. Verses one and three we sang collectively as third-graders. I remember this well because this particular Sunday, we third-graders were given our Bibles—a rite of passage—the very same Bible that we would be encouraged to bring to Sunday school that day and, going forward, to read, highlight, and memorize until that eventful day in the future, when as tenth-graders, we would be confirmed. From what I was told, we never had to open our Bible again, once confirmation took place.

> # Hardships
> ## often prepare
> # ordinary
> ## people
> ### for an
> ## extraordinary
> # destiny.
> ### C.S. Lewis

It was an honor to be chosen to sing the second stanza alone. I had mentally prepared for this moment. I had practiced my verse dozens of times standing on top of bales in the haymow. I would stretch my arms upward, as if directing the pigeon choir atop the rafters, singing with appropriate enthusiasm and gusto (as Cora Louise encouraged). I knew the words of verse two like I knew the lines to the Pledge of Allegiance.

As you may be aware, English poet and clergyman John Newton wrote "Amazing Grace" in 1779. Over the centuries, people have found great comfort in its message of forgiveness and redemption. It is possibly the most recognizable song in the English-speaking world—at least in the world of Lutherans.

The words I had memorized were these:

> *'Twas grace that taught my heart to fear,*
> *And grace my fears relieved.*
> *How precious did that grace appear*
> *The hour I first believed.*

However, as verse two quickly approached, I noticed that Mike Cirks' father, sitting in the fourth pew from the front, was sporting an orange tie with spectacularly wide white stripes. It was the most peculiar tie I had seen to date. And then, suddenly, it was time—time for my solo. As I began to belt out verse two, there was but one word in my head and that was SING. Thus I sang:

> *'Twas grace that taught me how to sing*
> *And sing and sing and sing*
> *While singing high and singing low,*
> *I sing just like a crow.*

It was a shame that John Newton was not present to hear the clever lyrics I created on the spot. Heidi later asked why I could not have come up with a better bird. "After all," she reminded me, "crows rarely make melodic, sweet sounds." I told her that it would have taken serious ingenuity to come up with a word that rhymed with a songbird such as chickadee, finch, or sparrow. In my opinion, *low* and *crow* worked just fine.

Since that day many years back, when the correct lyrics to a very familiar hymn were nowhere to be found, I've had my share of "dangers, toils, and snares." I am confident in this assertion: I am not alone. We live in a world that wants to trip us up and leave us battered and scarred. Let it be acknowledged that as human beings, we all have experienced one battle wound or another. Just because we are or have been wounded, this does not imply defeat. By God's grace, we are resilient, and most of us do have the tenacity to make something good come from life-interrupting events, which might be called "dangers, toils, and snares."

> *Through many dangers, toils, and snares*
> *I have already come;*
> *'Tis grace that brought me safe thus far*
> *And grace will lead me home.*

Indeed, "grace [has] brought me safe thus far"—through a cancer diagnosis, surgery, chemo, radiation, and a long arduous recovery—"and grace will lead me home."

MY STORY

August 31

Believe it or not, I am grateful that I was given the opportunity to experience cancer. Those views and values I claimed, prior to cancer, have been challenged, many changed. Dave and I have been showered with more love and grace than I could ever imagine. This journey has been endurable and I've never once felt alone.

September 4

My four BAD sessions of Chemo (Adriamycin/Cytoxan) are now over and I move on to 12 infusions of Taxol (supposedly easier on the system). I tend to be in a haze for 2-3 days, so if you called and I didn't make sense, call again. I will make an attempt to FOCUS!

Reggie, our cocker spaniel (8 months old), returned home yesterday. As many of you know, he spent the summer in Wisconsin with my brother. Reggie has matured a bit but yet as sweet and silly as when he departed in

94

June. It was so generous of them to care for him all summer long while I recovered from surgery and started treatment. Before I was diagnosed, I enrolled him in puppy kinder-garten here. He flunked. Or I flunked.

Nancy, my sister-in-law, was obviously a bit more diligent. While on his summer get-away, she enrolled Reggie in a class in Eleva, Wisconsin. He passed. I framed his diploma.

Right now, I believe that my attitude is critical regarding my health. I am thinking positive thoughts...

> *Everything is possible for him who believes.*
>
> Mark 9:23b

Please think positively about my recovery so a year from now, we can rejoice together.

September 7

We had such a lovely party at our home last night. 70+ people came to meet our charming four-month-old grandson, Leo. The evening was perfect; we sat around tables in the back yard and weren't consumed by mosquitoes. I am so grateful to Theresa, Loni and Mary who handled kitchen/wine details so I could sit and mingle.

I felt almost normal last night. Many hugs and encouraging words were shared. I am fortunate to be in a huge community of good people!

September 10

Quilting with girlfriends

What a fantastic 24 hours I've just experienced! Went out to Lynn's lake home in Minnesota and sewed/quilted with her and several other friends. I was able to be wigless and just me. Loved it. These are exceptional quilters and friends.

This morning, I got up early (5:30 a.m.) and sat on their dock and watched the sun rise while the loons sang. Thought I might have died and was experiencing heaven. Magnificently impressive. What fun to be a participant in the beginning of this new day.

Since cancer came into the picture, I think about my mortality more frequently than ever before—which I'm sure is part of the journey. This awesome journey; one adventure after the next. From birth to death, we are just one step away from heaven.

> God whispers in your soul and speaks to your mind. Sometimes when you don't take the time to listen, he has to throw a brick at you.
> It's your choice. Listen for the whisper or wait for the brick.
>
> author unknown

I will admit it. I was too busy to listen and the brick was necessary. God does have my attention now and I'm making an attempt at being as observant as possible.

MY STORY

September 16

Went in for infusion yesterday and a new chemo drug was administered (Taxol). My body tolerated it well.

Tomorrow I am speaking/singing at Trinity Lutheran in Crookston. My topic is CELE-BRATIONS OF LIFE and am excited to share at my home church at their WELCA Cluster 3 gathering. My pitch perfect, musical friend, Mary is coming with me (as she frequently does to talks where I intend to use music). She is one of the most tremendous gifts I've been given since arriving in Fargo in 1990. Not only is a super-duper friend to share cof-fee and bad movies with—she is also an ex-ceptional pianist and vocalist.

Back to the engagement tomorrow. Trinity is where I was baptized in 1960, sang my first solo, was confirmed in 1975 and married in 1981. My folks sat in the same pew for most of their married life (except when Mom sang in the choir loft up front). The funerals for both my parents were held there. I anticipate it feeling like holy ground. I will speak in the midst of a great cloud of witnesses that have gone before me.

I feel strong and confident that I am beating cancer and in the event that you are curious, I am still bald.

my father

My father was astounding.

Born May 16, 1917, he was named Oliver Randolph Christianson. From pictures I've seen, he was a beautiful baby. He grew into a handsome man, respected and admired by many, especially me, his youngest daughter.

When he was in eighth grade, his father (my grandpa) suffered a major coronary and died rather suddenly. So my father, the eldest of four children, quit school to help run the farm.

As each of my children turned 14, I looked at them with critical eyes and wondered if any of them might have the mettle to castrate baby pigs, throw hay bales, and plant and harvest a wheat field. It was painfully evident that my father's gene pool had skipped their tender generation. Most days, making a bed was beyond their capabilities (as well as mine, if truth be told).

My dad built the house I grew up in, seven miles west of Crookston. He was an architect, plumber, electrician, nail-driver and tile/carpet layer. Kitchen cabinets that he built in 1960 are still in use. I know of no other man that can do what he could do. If he didn't know how to do something, he'd read up on it and in short order, he would have it mastered. He would read *Popular Mechanics* and *Popular Science* from cover to cover, absorbing every page. Did I mention he had an eighth grade education?

Dad died on Thanksgiving Day of 1986. He was 69 years old. Our Isaac and Margot were four and three at the time. They have little memory of their Grandpa Randy. I was six months pregnant with

You're not **rich** until you have something that money **can't** buy . . .

Lucas when we received the call that Dad had suffered a lung embolism and was gone.

As a little kid, Lucas Oliver Wagner had an uncanny love of comic strips. The characters mesmerized him with the goofy things they said on printed page; Calvin and Hobbes was his favorite. Grandpa Randy loved comics. When his eyesight failed him, mom read the comic strips to him—telling him, slide by slide what was happening. And they would laugh, almost in harmony. Dad loved Beetle Bailey and Dennis the Menace. He also adored my mother!

I wish all my children would have a fond recollection of being embraced in Grandpa's strong arms. And, as Father's Day comes each year, I wish I could experience one last hug from this capable giant of a man. Each Father's Day, I find myself looking through the rows of cards trying to find the perfect card I would purchase for him if he were still here.

If I could, over coffee, I would tell him how much I appreciated his love for all of us six children. That the sacrifices he made for us did not go unnoticed. That we respected his work ethic and cherished the doting, sweet love he shared with mom for nearly 40 years. I would mention that as a little girl, I liked sitting by him in the pew on Sunday mornings. He would smile while looking up at mom, as she sang from the choir loft. It was seriously endearing for a daughter to witness. I hoped that someday a man would look at me with such affection.

I would also tell him that I was glad he led us in meal prayers and bedtime prayers.

I would tell him that breast cancer has made me a better, stronger person and I want him to be proud of me.

MY STORY

September 17

When I think about my story over the past three months, it seems surreal. Is it really possible that I have breast cancer? Is it possible that my chest is scarred and breast-less? I yet have 11 more sessions of chemo and then, the joy of several weeks of radiation therapy. All of this seems so crazy to imagine—and yet very real.

I'm not sure who originated the saying, but the following makes a lot of sense to me: It is not the circumstances of life that are most important, but your attitude toward them and how you permit them to affect you.

I don't know what circumstances you find yourself in right now, dear one. We are all struggling people, aren't we? Might I encourage you to not allow the little, insignificant things to affect you negatively. Bottom line is this—In God's vast knowledge, most of the things we deal with daily are pretty insignificant. Even cancer.

September 27

As much as I whine about my port being uncomfortable, it is of great benefit. Having my blood work drawn from the port negates having a vein tapped PLUS all infusion is done through this amazing little device.

For the first day of fall (or was it yesterday?), it's a stunning evening in Fargo. I should take the dogs for a nice walk around the neigh-borhood, but don't quite have the energy at this point. Tomorrow I will make it a priori-ty. This weekend's weather sounds PERFECT for September.

September 28

85 degrees this afternoon. Imagine that—and we are almost into October!

I feel so very blessed today. I have no pain. My chemo is remarkably easy on my system. I yet receive cards in the mail every day—with on-going encouragement/love/prayers from friends/family.

I don't deserve the tender grace & mercy I've received. I am humbled by the concern shown by many.

This morning I dropped Reggie (cocker spaniel) off for a haircut at the groomer. She asked what I had in mind for his trim. I explained that I used to groom my own cockers and presently am undergoing chemo and just don't have the energy to trim him myself. She asked what my prognosis was. Good question.

So, what can I say? I really don't know. My hope is that the chemo treatments are effectively killing off any remaining cancer cells in my body. But how does one know?

God knows. He has all my days planned out for me. Which is good, since I have a difficult time ordering my days myself.

Chemo on Friday.

September 30

Losing Eyebrows

Several weeks back my entry title was LOSING HAIR. Today it is: LOSING EYEBROWS. This evening I went to the store and purchased a "brow enhancer" pencil which is just the ticket for my predicament. Due to meds, I'm also dealing with severely dry lips—so I picked up Burt's Bees lip balm. Tomorrow I shall have enhanced brows and luscious lips—all will be amazed.

As crazy as it sounds, at the store I walked up and down the shampoo aisle dreaming of the day I would require this product again. How my silly mind works! Let's blame it on the chemo.

Today was infusion day. It went great. Effortless; tonight I am feeling energetic. I told Dave this and he mentioned that as he glanced at me from a distance at the store, I appeared very tired. So much for feeling well! I've always appreciated his honesty—

but my vanity does not find joy hearing I look tired.

I took a two hour nap this afternoon. Felt invigorating.

Today I read a prayer written by Stormie Omartian:

Lord, show me what You want me to do today to be a blessing to others. I don't want to be so wrapped up in my own life that I don't see the opportunity for ministering Your life to those around me. Show me what You want me to do and enable me to do it. Give me all I need to minister life, hope, help, and healing to others. Make me to be one of Your faithful intercessors, and teach me how to pray in power. Help me to make a big difference in the world because You are working through me to touch lives for Your glory. May my greatest treasure always be in serving You.

AMEN

There you go. I hope to be serving God with my last breath—with or without eyebrows.

May you have the BEST weekend ever. The Fargo weather sounds unseasonably warm and sensational for the next few days. I hope to get out and ride my bike. As my friend, Scott would say at the conclusion of any conversation, "You choose to have a good day." Just do it.

October 5

Just to get this straight...

My son is marrying Melissa in April. Melissa's mother is Wendy. Wendy is a faithful, Godly woman and she has been sending me on-going support and encouragement. I think I've actually visited with Wendy (in the flesh) but once and that was years ago when our sons were running in a Cross Country meet. Little did we know then, that her daughter and my son would fall in love and marry one day. But, we've become fast friends.

Wendy suggested I read 2 Corinthians 8-10. Lovely words:

> *Three times I begged the Lord to make this suffering go away. But he replied, "My gift of undeserved grace is all you need. My power is strongest when you are weak." So if Christ keeps giving me his power, I will gladly brag about how weak I am. Yes, I am glad to be weak or insulted or mistreated or to have troubles and sufferings, if it is for Christ. Because when I am weak, I am strong.*

Yes, I will admit it. I have done my share of begging and pleading that this time of trial be brief (after all, Lord, kindly remember that I am a busy woman). However, whatever is to be, I will deal with it. Each day brings its share of challenges, but I trust all will be well.

Fargo weather is hot. Today it was the mid 80s—and this is October! I am not complaining—just wishing I could spend the day under a tree, in a park perhaps, with a good book. You too?

When I am feeling vulnerable and a bit cheated out of the "good life" (what does that look like??), I am reminded that this world is not our home and that we shouldn't get too comfortable. I find comfort in that.

May you sense undeserved grace beyond measure in the days ahead. You are loved.

October 9

My 51st Birthday!

51 years ago today, Audrey gave birth to her "sweet" baby girl, Kim. I am so thankful that I was part of the bigger picture...Mom & Dad thought they were all done having kiddos after Heidi arrived. 11 months later I showed up and life was never quite the same in the Christianson home. We would not want to be bored, ever.

I am feeling well. Crazy stuff and hard to believe. But really feeling strong after each chemo session of Taxol. I had my 4th Taxol treatment on Friday and only have 8 to go!

So, on this rainy, fall day in Fargo, as I celebrate my birthday—I am so thankful that each of you plays a special role in my life.

Since cancer entered the picture, I am much more aware of how sacred each day is and how fortunate I am to have cheerleaders in place to offer their encouragement. You all make my present journey joyful!

I am thankful for another birthday. For the joy of hearing from all my kids (even Skyping with little Leo, who is so very sweet and handsome, of course). I am thankful for every friend who is concerned about me.

all will
be well

I watched her die. Well, almost. My mother, the infamous pea-picker, took her own sweet time when it came to dying.

On the concentrated care flow sheet and attached notes attained from Hospice of the Red River Valley, this was noted of Audrey Christianson's last moments:

> Arrived at patient's house. Patient
> in hospital bed in living room.
> Daughters Pat and Heidi are at

If there ever
comes a day
when we can't be
together,
keep
me in your
heart.
I'll stay there
forever.

A.A. Milne, Winnie-the-Pooh

bedside. Patient's hand is very dusky.
Unable to hear blood pressure.
Morphine (10 mg) breaker given.
Patient is using stomach muscles
to breathe. Feet mottling. No blood
pressure heard. Labored breathing.
10:45 p.m. patient's eyes opened.
Response more of a gasp. Family
at bedside. 10:50 p.m. no response.
No heartbeat. TOD 10:50 p.m.
Coroner was notified of death. Called
Stenshoel's Funeral Home. Destroyed
patient meds per HRRV protocol. 12
a.m. funeral home arrived to remove
body. 12:30 a.m. family is doing OK—
grieving appropriately. OFF duty.

NOTE: Peaceful death. Daughters Pat
and Heidi and granddaughter Randi
at bedside at time of death.

My Norwegian mother had been diagnosed with
pancreatic cancer in October of 2006.

The patient developed progressive
weight loss since October 2006. She

lost 15 pounds. She became jaundiced mid-October 2006. She was admitted to the hospital on 10/25/06. The W/U was suspicious for a tumor of the head of the pancreas. She had an ERCP by Dr. Deshpande on 10/26/06 having a plastic stent placed in the common bile duct. Brushings were obtained showing atypical cells non-diagnostic of malignancy. The jaundice has progressively resolved.

A repeated endoscopic US by Dr. Lai identified a tumor in the head of the pancreas. It encases the SMA, SMV and portal vein. It abuts the celiac artery. The stent was visualized. There was 1 enlarged LN near the pancreatic head very suspicious for metastasis. A needle biopsy of the mass was performed and recovered Aden carcinoma. Since she has a T4 lesion she was felt unresectable. Patient was put on 2 weeks of chemo but experienced severe sores in the mouth and diarrhea. She declined to

take a second cycle due to the side
effects. Patient has developed LE
edema, which is bothersome.

Chart documentation
MeritCare Hospital
Fargo, North Dakota

As noted, after a two-week stint of oral chemo medications that made her frightfully ill, she opted out. Her oncologist was forthright—something we all appreciated. Audrey Christianson was informed she had six months to a year to live.

This was about the time that Carnegie Mellon University computer science professor Randy Pausch spoke on "Really Achieving Your Childhood Dreams," also referred to as "The Last Lecture." Pausch shared his talk on September 18, 2007, alternating between humor, insights into computer science and engineering, interaction with other people, and life's lessons—along with performing push-ups on stage. It was an overnight sensation and the basis for a *New York Times* best-selling

> Distance between two hearts is not an obstacle; rather a beautiful reminder of just how strong true love can be...

book called *The Last Lecture*, co-authored with *Wall Street Journal* reporter Jeffrey Zaslow.

Pausch's talk was a part of an ongoing series of lectures in which top individuals in academia were asked to think deeply about what mattered to them, and then give a hypothetical "final talk"— i.e., "What wisdom would you try to impart to the world if you knew it was your last chance?"

Randy Pausch was diagnosed with terminal pancreatic cancer on September 19, 2006, only weeks prior to my mother's terminal diagnosis. Mom eagerly watched the coverage given to this man and waited, with many of us, to hear of his demise. It was actually almost two years before he died. Surrounded by his loving family, he passed away on July 25, 2008.

My mother was an anxious soul. My father, the love of her life, died on Thanksgiving Day of 1986, and she grew weary from the many years of separation. I believe she experienced times of euphoric anticipation at the thought that she had only months, perhaps weeks, before she would again be in the arms of the man of her dreams. Forget the arms of Jesus; at this time she was thinking of my dad!

Things didn't move along quite as she hoped. My pea-picker mother was admitted to hospice care on December 3, 2007. She died over two years later—January 25, 2009.

I inherited her journals. Years and years of journals. The first we found was from 1945, the year she and Dad married.

As illness invaded her life, her world became smaller and smaller—as did her penmanship. Her journal entries reflected her frustration with a body growing increasingly dependent on medication and unable to maintain normal functions. Her journals also reflected her longing to "go home." *Home* to her was heaven, and at this point, to my mother, most days felt like heaven was a million miles away.

Ultimately, she didn't take much time to "go home" after I left her home in Crookston to drive back to Fargo that bitterly cold Sunday evening in January. Days of maintaining a vigil at her deathbed had left me threadbare, and I longed for one night in my own bed. As I was about to depart, I kissed her forehead and whispered in her ear, "I'll be back early tomorrow morning, Mom. Wait for me."

Surely she would wait for me. After all, I was her favorite.

She didn't wait. But I *would* see her again.

Just hours after having a bilateral mastectomy, entranced in the glory of a morphine drip, I found myself all alone in a hospital room in the middle of the night. Except for the occasional landing of the emergency helicopter outside and the beeping of my IV drip, the room was very quiet and eerily dark.

She touched my arm. Before I even opened my eyes, I could smell her. I recognized Mom's favorite perfume, Topaze.

This particular fragrance was launched in 1959 and sold exclusively through AVON. June Lindell, Mom's AVON lady, had introduced this "rare fragrant gem" to my farm-wife mother. I was listening to their conversation while eating a chocolate chip cookie, yet warm from the oven. The two of them sat at the kitchen table on the farm, enjoying a cup of coffee as June read from its label, "Audrey, notice the top notes are aldehydes, coriander, peach, bergamot, and lemon; middle notes are carnation, iris, jasmine, ylang-ylang, lily-of-the-valley, and rose; base notes are sandalwood, tonka bean, amber, benzoin, civet, and vetiver." Impressed with the musicality of this floral fragrance, Mom, I believe, was convinced that Topaze was created just for her.

That night in my hospital room, I felt her touch, smelled her fragrance, and immediately knew it was her.

I glanced at the chair beside the window and there she was; oddly, I was not surprised. I opened my eyes, and in the dark I could sense her smiling at me, her hand still touching my arm. The woman who sat beside me was beautiful and a much younger version of my mother. There was no sign of a ravaging cancer invading her. Perfect and whole, she was sitting in my room! My arm was covered with goose bumps.

She spoke only four words: "All will be well." Ah! To hear her voice again! I had forgotten its sweetness.

"But, Mom," I argued, "do you know I have cancer? This is real, and I have no control over this. Not sure if I can do this . . . or do it well." I was babbling.

She removed her hand from my arm and repeated, "All will be well."

I closed my eyes, relishing the fact that she had come to visit, forgetting that she had come a very long way to sojourn with me (heaven is not exactly next door, is it?).

I am unsure how long I rested. But when I awoke, her touch was gone. I opened my eyes, searching for her face, realizing that the chair was now empty. I sniffed the air. Her scent was absent. And so was she.

I sobbed as I had not done since the early days of my diagnosis. I cried, not because my girls had been surgically removed from my chest, but because my mother had left my hospital room without saying a proper goodbye.

Even so, as it turned out, my mother was right. All would be well.

October 15

Great Friends!

Our Church Ladies group met last night. Diane had us over to her home for lasagna and marvelous conversation. It was a perfect evening of sharing as SISTERS. The theme of the gathering was pink—and I took home lots of wonderful gifts...pink socks, pink mugs, pink nail polish, pink scarf. It felt like Christmas.

We shared all kinds of things regarding our families, our future plans, caught up on latest relationships (the good, bad and ugly). The only thing missing was the slumber party. Perhaps next time.

I had my weekly Taxol infusion yesterday morning. It went fine. My port had not worked well the previous week, but yesterday it worked PERFECTLY. It was a relief. I'm starting to like that little gadget under my skin. Only seven more chemo treatments to go.

So now that I am into year 51, I best get busy accomplishing a few things. I have made a list of things to do around the house today. Every Saturday morning as I was growing up, Mom would give us a list of chores to complete. The sooner we finished our list (& she would make sure we actually DID what we crossed off our list), the sooner we could get out to the barn to ride horses, or do something else desirable. I should make more lists—it appears that I accomplish very little.

Have a beautiful weekend, dear one. Might I encourage you to appreciate today. As my "sisters" reminded me last night, no one is guaranteed tomorrow. But, look—we awoke up to a beautiful fall morning in Fargo. Grand—enjoy today. God is good.

October 19

Billboard

So, I sat at the stop light longer than necessary to see if it's true. And yes, it is true.
Eventually the rotating billboard that lit the
sky by DOOLITTLES, popped up with my BIG
face on it. One doesn't realize how large one
is until seen on a billboard.

It says, "Celebrate" view my victory story at
cancer.sanfordhealth.org with my monster
big face on it. Actually, this is perfect timing
with Halloween right around the corner (too
bad I couldn't follow the haunted corn maze
advertisement).

Tonight when I stopped at the grocery store
on the way home from praise band practice,
a man asked me if I was the same person
as the one on the billboard. Hard to deny. I
wanted to say, "Nope, that's my twin sister
who has breast cancer—not me."

Stage 3 breast cancer. This is reality.

Friends keep telling me that I need to take this time, right now, to heal and beat this disease. What if I can't? What if all the chemo and radiation and awesome work of brilliant doctors is not enough? What if God has other plans for me?

I received the following from a friend today (in a book called JESUS CALLING):

Trust Me and refuse to worry, for I am your Strength and Song. You are feeling wobbly this morning, looking at difficult times looming ahead, measuring them against your own strength. However, they are not today's tasks—or even tomorrow's. So leave them in the future and come home to the present, where you will find Me waiting for you. Since I am your Strength I can empower you to handle each task as it comes. Because I am your Song, I can give you Joy as you work alongside Me.

MY STORY

Keep bringing your mind back to the present moment. Among all My creatures, only humans can anticipate future events. This ability is a blessing, but it becomes a curse whenever it is misused. If you use your magnificent mind to worry about tomorrow, you cloak yourself in dark unbelief. However, when the hope of heaven fills your thoughts, the Light of My Presence envelops you. Though heaven is future, it is also present tense. As you walk in the Light with Me, you have one foot on earth and one foot in heaven.

To be honest, I am feeling a little wobbly, looking at difficult things that lie ahead. Again on Friday I will have poison pumped into my veins—hoping the bad cells are killed off and good cells remain; such a conflicting science.

October 30

Lab tests on Thursday determined that my white blood cells are declining—which is pretty typical. The last three weeks have seen white cells go from 2,500 to 1,800 (normal is 2,250 – 7,700). If it drops below 1,500, I need to postpone chemo and my oncologist is hopeful that won't happen. I had an injection of Neupogen yesterday, which burned. This is to boost my bone marrow/white count production. It causes my bones to ache terribly.

I have more fatigue than I've experienced in the past. I've taken several naps the last 48 hours. I feel like an old, worn out lady.

My dear friend Mary stopped over this afternoon with a pot of Gerbera Daisies to cheer me up. We had a cup of coffee and it was good to have someone to talk to. She is a beautiful friend.

Again, cancer has sharpened my focus on what is really important about life. If it was suggested I had six months to live, I would do things a bit different. How about you?

P.S. Rejoice with me...my hair is growing back! I see eyebrows returning and the hair on my head is a whopping 1/4 inch long.

November 4

My cancer adventure!

I was asked to speak to the students at Fisher (MN) public school this week regarding my breast cancer journey. The students were extremely well-behaved and it was easy to engage them (& at the end of their school day!). My niece, Hannah and her group of PEER MENTORS orchestrated an amazing event (plus a fund raiser for me). I was deeply touched by their generosity to an unknown woman dealing with breast cancer. There are AMAZING young people in Fisher!

I was sent home with a plastic pumpkin full of little messages from many of the students.

Several of their notes are so darn cute! Examples from young children, obviously:

I hope you get better cause I feal so bad. I feal really really really really really really bad.

Alexis

There's a drawing at the bottom of a stick person on a hospital bed which looks like baby Jesus in the manger and labeled: Mrs. Wagner)

I think it is so sad to have cancer. My grandpa had cancer and all I would like to say to you is...good luck. Fight the cancer. Get better soon.

Rylie

I am sorry that you have bress canser. I wish you wod fel better.

Love Libby

Libby and Mrs. Kim Wagner are stick people on the top of the note. Libby stickgirl has hair. Mrs. Kim Wagner stickgirl is bald.

*I hope you feel bedder. Don't loose
the hope. You have supporting friends,
family & even strangers you don't even
know (like me) still wish you the best.*

*Don't think of cancer as something
bad. Think of it as an adventure!*
                                    Hellanna

Now how awesome is this? I will enjoy reading these notes of encouragement for days! I
love Hellanna's comment that I should think
of cancer as an adventure! COOL thought,
little friend.

November 4

An extra treat! My kind friends, Don and Jennifer sent me a beautiful box of Harry and David's Honeycrisp apples. It's like these were picked off the tree the day they arrived. Absolutely yummy! What makes this gift extra special is that Jennifer dealt with breast cancer a few years back and has offered me great encouragement. Goodness, see how lucky I am? I find hope in hearing from survivors.

I am almost up to 10,000 visitors to this site. Simply incredible. Keep the positive vibes coming my way; your prayers and encouragement keep me going. I love each of you!

asking

Why is it so difficult to ask for what we need?

I recall asking for many things as a little girl—more toys, more dessert, my own bedroom.

As I grew, my "asks" (as they often say in the world of marketing and development) became bolder and more demanding: I want a new horse, and then . . . I need a new saddle for my new horse. I want a new boyfriend. I want the lead in the high school musical. It was no longer, "May I please have another dessert?" My "May I . . . ?" changed to "I want and I need . . ."

When my son Isaac was soon to turn eight, he asked for a pup tent. Not just *any* pup tent. He wanted it domed, with water-resistant flooring, a window, and large enough for two people. Actually, what he really wanted was for it to be large enough to allow for a small TV to be strung from the house so he could watch TV at his leisure (at eight!), eat popcorn, and sleep in a sleeping bag in the backyard, away from his three younger siblings.

We had already purchased Isaac's birthday gift by the time he made his ask. We reminded him that we weren't made of money and that he'd have to be satisfied with what we had already wrapped. He was persistent. At bedtime prayers, Isaac

Enjoy the little things, for one day you may look back and realize they were the big things.

Robert Brault

closed his eyes and asked again, "God. This is Isaac. We live in Fargo and I am in third grade. My birthday is tomorrow, and I would like a red pup tent." He asked. There—simple; a quick birthday request.

So often we hesitate to ask—to ask for what our heart is yearning for. It might be something simple, like a kid's pup tent. It might be a big request, like "Please give me healing from my breast cancer." Regardless, it's just asking.

That particular June night, the night before Isaac's eighth birthday, the weather grew stormy. Strong winds and heavy rain zigzagged haphazardly. By morning the storm had passed, and we welcomed sunshine—a perfect beginning to the special day.

As Dave and I sipped our morning coffee at the kitchen table, I pulled open the patio blinds. Crazy as it sounds, what did we discover on our patio that late spring morning? A green, domed, nylon pup tent. It had blown from someone else's yard straight into the Wagners' backyard.

As you can imagine, Isaac was simply elated. We assured our young son that it really was not meant for him and that we intended to locate the rightful owner.

We tied the tent to our mailbox and put a sign on it: BLEW INTO OUR BACKYARD. IF THIS IS YOURS, TAKE IT HOME.

One week later, no one had claimed it. That's how Isaac got a pup tent the summer he turned eight—he simply asked for it.

What did I learn from this? I learned that we have to be very specific as to how we ask and what we ask for. If we are really to get our heart's desire, it will arrive on its own terms. And if we pay close attention, it just might land in our own backyard.

What am I asking for? A simple thing. Time. Right now, that's all I need.

Don't be **afraid** of
death;
Be afraid of an
unlived life.
You don't have to
live forever,
You just have
to live.

November 12

Possibilities

Only three more chemo treatments to go. CELEBRATE with me!

I recently read a sweet little devotion called BIRTHING PAINS written by Hope Lyda.

> *This is the year. My friends and I have felt that this could be the year we do more than merely contemplate and mull over our ideas. This could be the time in our lives when we put our ideas out into the world and see what can come of them.*
>
> *Each day you must say to yourself, today I am going to begin.*

I have all these crazy, creative ideas in my head and am fearful that that's where they will stay. I should take the advice of many, a bit more seriously, and let the story of my recent journey see the light of day. It's been an interesting time in my life. So, what is holding me back from pushing my dreams forward?

Must remember to ask God what his intentions are for me. It's so easy to tell him how I believe my journey should play out. He must find it amusing—for me to think that I have it all figured out—and I have the audacity to tell him so!

Today I am thankful for the many opportunities that present themselves. I hope I am wise enough to see them as opportunities.

November 20

Sporting my nifty wig, I spoke/sang this morning at Sand Hill Lutheran Church (rural Climax, MN) at their worship service. It was marvelous! Mary drove with from Fargo and she played piano and sang duets on several pieces.

It is getting easier to share my cancer story with others. So many have been down this path before me. I am all the stronger because of having to go through this.

Only two more chemo treatments to go! I have chemo on Black Friday morning—so my intentions are to get up & shop with the crazy people at midnight and arrive at the Roger Maris Cancer Center in time for a good long snooze. How fun does that sound?

Our eldest, Isaac is flying in on Tuesday evening. He will be with us over Thanksgiving and will fly back to Portland Friday morning. He is the last of our kids to make it home since I was diagnosed. I look forward to having him home with us.

We have not been told anything definitive about when radiation will begin. Imagine that information will be shared in the upcoming weeks. For now, I'm just so grateful for each new day.

> *Can you view a recent loss or struggle as a blessing? Do you see how your deconstruction is leading to the rebuilding of faith and hope? The new thing God is creating in your life will lead you forward. Trust in that.*
>
> Hope Lyda

November 25

Thanksgiving at the Wagner household resulted in a red-letter day. All went magnificently well.

We had worship service at our church on Wednesday evening and Thanksgiving morning Dave and I helped with the music at Riverview Place (my employer).

MY STORY

My sister Pat has been with us this week. She has been remarkable! Of all my siblings, she has jumped at every opportunity to assist me. Our son Isaac flew in Tuesday night from Portland, OR. So, along with our church friend Esther we had only five for Thanksgiving lunch. We all ate our fill of turkey, dressing, potatoes, sweet potato casserole, lefse, pumpkin pie, etc. etc. Outrageous to think that people are hungry in this country when we all ate far too much.

Talked to my sister Heidi in Mesa. She was excited about the lefse I mailed from Fargo. I just wish I could have shared the meal with her and her kids, as well. That would have been PERFECT.

As many of you may recall, my father Randy died on Thanksgiving Day in 1986. Thanksgiving will never be the same.

No BLACK FRIDAY shopping for me. I had blood draw, doctor visit and chemo this morning—Neupogen shots on Saturday. Only one more chemo treatment to follow on Dec. 2.

Dave and I have our 30th anniversary on Nov. 28. Where did those years go? We hope to go out for dinner on Sunday night to celebrate, as Monday may be busy. Dave continues to be my dearest friend and faithful partner in this life. As much as we irritate each other, there is no one I'd rather be with (most of the time).

Dave asked me last week what was the thing I feared the most regarding cancer. I said, "Dying from it." And then he asked what was the best thing about cancer? I thought for a moment and replied, "The possibility of dying from it." Heaven is ok.

Since we are to embark on another cold, dark, snowy North Dakota winter, singing praises at the feet of Jesus in the warmth of heaven seems very attractive to me. Whenever that may be.

Sweet friends, all is good and I am so thankful for each of you.

the bitch

Breast cancer.

Maybe I was dreaming.

"What does it look like?" I asked.

"It looks like a bitch," the doctor said.

"A bitch? The cancer looks like a bitch? What does that mean?" I asked.

"It means," he replied choosing his words deliberately, "we use this word when *it* could potentially kill you."

Dream or no dream, my cancer was ugly. I was fifty years old. I had a three-month-old grandson. My initial fear was that I would not have enough time with little Leo. I rationalized, *What would be "enough" time? Five years? Ten or twenty years?* Surely our all-loving, gracious Heavenly Father would allow me *enough* time, whatever that looked like from His perspective.

Besides Leo, there was my eldest son, Isaac. Isaac had not yet proposed to beautiful Melissa. It was only a matter of time. Would

I be here to participate in their wedding? If not, would they miss me? Would they raise their wine glasses and say, "She should have made it to this party, but the bitch killed her . . ."

I read everything I could get my hands on: diagnostic imaging reports, lab reports, pathology reports, and surgical reports. Everything. I wanted to know everything.

On April 14, 2011, radiologist William F. Wosick noted in his report, "Suspicious abnormality. Two dominant (1.9 cm and 4.0 cm) cysts—lower/outer quadrant of right breast—with an adjacent incompletely circumscribed 13 mm non-cystic nodule or mass—indeterminate." When I read it, I knew exactly what it was. Odd, they didn't ask me. I would have gladly explained it in comprehensible terms. Quite simply, what he was looking at was . . . a bitch.

The surgical biopsy on June 8th determined the bitch to be a 5.5 cm cancerous tumor. No clean margins. On July 1, eight of eleven lymph nodes were cancerous. But according to the surgical report from stellar breast surgeon Dr. Michael Bouton, "Estimated blood loss for the procedures was 100 ml. No complications. Sponge and instrument counts were correct. Patient was transferred to recovery room in stable condition."

Breast-less, but stable. Thank God all the sponges were accounted for.

I was released from the hospital less than twenty-four hours after having a bilateral mastectomy. The girls were gone. Dr. Bouton made his Saturday morning rounds and stopped in to unwind the supportive Ace wrap and to remind me, "Things will be different now." He was very kind. After removing the wrap, he asked if I wanted time to be "alone."

For what? To ponder how "different" things were, now that the breasts that nursed four babies were in the lab, floating in trays of formaldehyde?

Yes, things were certainly different. My chest had two eight-inch wounds covered by Steri-Strips. I asked Dr. Bouton how the Ace wrap was applied

Only God can turn a **MESS** into a message, a **TEST** into a testimony, a **TRIAL** into a triumph, a **VICTIM** into a victory.

during surgery. He explained that the operating team sits the patient up and proceeds to wrap up the chest. The visual I had was not attractive. I wanted to apologize in the event that I had drooled or gagged on the intubation tube as they sat me up and wrapped me up to resemble a mummy. I said nothing.

I returned home with the narcotic pain reliever Oxy-Contin (oxycodone). I was determined to gain back my strength and heal. I was anxious to participate in little Leo's first birthday party and longed to hear Isaac speak marriage vows to his beloved, Melissa.

Another year. God, if you are listening, please give me another year.

December 4

WOOHOO! Last chemo took place on Friday. I have not experienced the fatigue and bone aches I have over past weekends (no Neupogin shot). I am indebted to many.

Got to thinking about the many women that experience breast cancer, go through surgery and treatment, end up with a reoccurrence and end up dying from this disease. Could be me. But for now, I rejoice in the little miracles that I've experienced.

To be frank, I will miss my Friday appointments at the infusion center. I know many of the nurses by name (as they know me) and looked forward to visiting with them. I have heard about their cats, dogs, children, and husbands. Some nurses are chatty; some are quiet. I've had the opportunity to share bits and pieces of my life and my faith with many.

There is one beautiful nurse with striking auburn curly hair. I loved being assigned to her; I told her that I hoped my hair would return looking just like hers. Must tell you, my hair is nearly a WHOLE inch in length. Sadly, it is not auburn or curly. It is very grey and very straight. But, hair—nonetheless. Actually, it's extremely soft (like a newborn kitten). I may just leave it grey and keep it short like Jamie Lee Curtis. No one can tell me she is not glamorous with her short, grey hair.

I am working on a breast cancer survivor book involving women willing to share their stories. I have offered to help them write their narrative, if they should desire and visited with several of them last night.

Incredible women! Every one of us has a different story but all share much in common. This is not a path any of us would have chosen for ourselves—but grateful to be a part of the journey together. We have great synergy all together—like we are part of a mighty army.

It is December 4 in Fargo. No snow on the ground. I am filled with the assurance that our wonderful God knows the perfect time to send the snowflakes as well as the healing for breast-less bodies like mine. I certainly don't feel worthy of all the prayers sent on my behalf, but will be forever grateful.

December 20

Only days until Christmas. And, I get to start radiation. This will continue for six weeks, ending January 31. Every day of the week (no weekends). There really is nothing to it—the easiest thing I've had to do so far.

Son, Lucas (Irvine, CA) flew home tonight. Tomorrow our youngest, Abram will arrive from Ann Arbor, MI. It will be wonderful having them both home for Christmas. Our two eldest, Isaac and Margot, are unable to get home. Packages were mailed and I will miss them terribly. This is the first Christmas that we won't all be together.

I've retired my wig. My hair is almost an inch long and it feels quite liberating to go without cap or wig. It's the authentic me, folks. Like it or not! I didn't say that I look glamorous—just comfortable.

It has become customary in recent years, for Dave and I to publish our Christmas letter in February. So, don't be looking for our greeting to arrive anytime soon...

However, we do wish each of you a Christmas filled with the fondest of memories and joy beyond belief. God's richest blessings to each of you.

And as always, you are adored.

December 26

Merry Christmas!

Christmas Eve we had church and then went to our friend, Esther's for dinner, gift sharing and card playing. MUCH fun! Then we headed over to my brother, Mark's home. Their two youngest, Cody and Kailey are home and it's been years since the cousins got together. All of these goofy kids have turned into great adults.

Christmas day we put steaks on the grill. We had four guests join us (some of our favorite people). It was a quiet, restful day—except when all three dogs were let out of their kennels and they flew around the living room & kitchen like they were on fire. Can't imagine another Christmas in the near future where we will be grilling, have no snow and it be warm enough to open windows. We aren't complaining!

I finished my first week of radiation. Not much to it; I haven't experienced any discomfort relating to it. The technicians are all exceptionally kind. All those working in Oncology are the BEST.

I'm continuing to gather stories from area breast cancer survivors. These women are astounding. I count myself fortunate to be able to visit with them. All are encouraging. Beautiful people!

Another new year is almost here. How can we make a difference yet in this year? I'm asking God to bless each of you in a remarkable way so you sense how much he loves you. He truly is AWESOME and I am thankful to know and to trust him. I have never felt alone in the past six months since being diagnosed. Rejoice!

if not now, when?

When your gifts and passion align, therein lies your purpose.

Renee Rongen

In my opinion, Renee Rongen is one of the finest motivational humorists in the speaking world today. Besides being a hilarious speaker, she is an award-winning author, a successful entrepreneur, a fabulous wife and mother, and my dear friend. We have known each other since kindergarten, and it is only by the grace of God that we lived to graduate from high school. As teenagers, we'd meet at a designated spot and ride our horses. After confirming that saddle cinches were tight, we'd give our horses a swift kick of encouragement and race across a stubble field at full speed, feeling exhilarated and invincible. The power of this magnificent beast, galloping in long strides beneath me, took my breath away. It was risky, but liberating!

Renee *gets* life. Many years back, I spent a morning with her at her rural home, drinking coffee and reminiscing. She pointed out that some of the boards on her kitchen walls and ceiling had come from a barn that was being demolished. These pieces, tattered and worn, featured amazing character. It

was incredible to see that years of mighty winds, rain, and snowstorms had only made them more seasoned and beautiful. It the midst of our chatting about the woodwork, Renee, in her typical direct fashion, asked, "So, girlfriend, what's keeping you from pursuing the career you've always wanted? You want to be a professional speaker, right?"

Making no sense whatsoever, I tried to justify my many excuses. Noting her impatience, I finally stammered, "But, Renee, it's risky and I don't want to fail."

"Kim, what's your purpose? Why are you *here*?" She gave me one of her astute looks and said assuredly, "You know you have the gifts you need to work this business and to be successful. I'm not telling you something you haven't already figured out, right? You do know who is standing in your way, don't

Don't be **afraid** to fail. Be afraid not to **try**.

you?" She paused, refilling our coffee cups. "It's *you*, Sweet Pea. Only you, Hon."

Me? In my own way? Though I was alone in my car, the return trip to Fargo was *not* quiet as I tried to make sense of this revelation. The ongoing chatter of voices in my head was deafening. I tried to silence them, but they were relentless and conflicting, and they would not be hushed . . . for months.

And then there was that conversation with Pam, one of my co-workers, who had been diagnosed with cancer a couple months before I received my diagnosis. We shared our experiences of the nasty

side effects of chemo and the burning sensations of radiation. Different drug protocols for different types of cancer—but many similarities. While comparing notes, we applauded our little victories and struggled with the unrelenting fierceness of this disease, as only cancer sisters can. We were each other's cheerleader; we just didn't have the pompoms to wave. Our mantra: "Together—we will beat the beast!"

One day in early April when there was yet snow on the ground, I stopped at her home to pass along greetings from several of our co-workers. "Everyone misses you, Pam." Then, quickly changing topics, "Hey! You won't believe this, but I'm actually thinking of submitting my resignation letter."

In the past, we had talked at length about my desire to quit my fundraising job and pursue full-time speaking. In a soft, tired voice she whispered, "Kim, if not now, when?"

I had excuses. "Perhaps once we have more financial resources. The speaking business can be risky," I reminded her. She nodded. "Maybe when I know that I have several months of solid gigs booked, then I could resign from my position with the foundation. Maybe if Dave got a big raise at the church and we didn't have so much debt." Pam smiled and nodded again. *Like that might happen.*

"Kim, we would have never had babies if we had waited for money to be in place. And would you have ever learned to drive if you knew at the time how dangerous it could be?" Breathless, she paused to rest. "There are so many things I should have just done—but the timing wasn't right. Like you, I put things off. Dumb."

"So what things do you wish you would have done, Pamela? Really—are there things you wish you would have done?"

She took a deep breath, "Maybe. But that's water under the bridge."

She was obviously tired; exhaustion was etched on her face. This wasn't a topic I should have brought up. We could be talking about spring coming, the days warming up, and garden planting. Or conceivably, we should be talking about her impending death. Hospice had delivered a bed to her home, medication was required to keep her comfortable, and she was, obviously, running out of time. A conversation pertaining to time and upcoming opportunities seemed irrelevant, given the circumstances.

Pam never used the word "terminal" when talking about her illness. That would imply that the "beast" was going to win. I knew—and of course Pam knew—that she was dying of esophageal cancer, but "terminal" was just too *final* of a word for either of us to use.

If you start paying **attention** to the voice in your head that's telling you it's **time** to change your life, it might let you **sleep at night.**

Even so, she asked me that day, "You will sing for my funeral?" I nodded and said, "Of course I will sing."

Her obituary read:

> *Pamela Jean Mathern, 57, passed away on Saturday, April 20, 2013, at her home under the care of Hospice of the Red River Valley, after a very brave and courageous, almost three-year battle with cancer.*

That conversation—"If not now, when?"—was the last one I had with Pam.

The meaning of life is to find your gift. The purpose of life is to give it away.

Pablo Picasso

It took me another year and a half, but in the fall of 2014, I resigned from the rewarding, stable development position I thoroughly enjoyed and jumped into the unknown territory of self-employment. I won't say I haven't had moments of uncertainly, but it has been worth every risk, every challenge.

I speak full-time now—or as "full-time" as I want to be. I have been given an opportunity to use my gifts and my passion to encourage, to engage, and to share laughter and life's lessons with people across the nation. Incidentally, it has been during times of deepest grief, heartache, pain, and questioning that I have learned life's greatest intangible lessons. Just as orphan Annie belts out that "the sun will come out tomorrow," there are times when *today* doesn't make any sense. Hopefully, if we're given the opportunity to experience it, *tomorrow* will.

In my speaking, I frequently tell people about Pam and her marvelous sense of humor, her wisdom, and her unfailing courage. I am thankful to God for giving me the opportunity to share in a small part of her life.

January 6

I am finishing week #3 of radiation. Half done. It appears to be going well. No major sunburn yet—and I'm feeling fine, though fatigued. Very normal, I've been told.

I am participating in a trial study following radiation. It will be a Metformin study—unknown if I am receiving the real deal or placebo.

And, wonder of wonders, the BACHELOR is back on Monday nights. Several friends want to start another Beth Moore study and have expressed interest in Monday nights. How can I possibly give up the BACHELOR? I can't even discuss the show without capitalizing it. Quite certain there's a bit of unwarranted reverence placed on this. Need I say more?

We have experienced a balmy December and thus far in January, the same. Yesterday we had temps in the high 50s—unknown for North Dakota (we broke a 30-year record high). Our kids were hoping for a white Christmas when they were home. No such luck. I am reminded that this will make our winter much shorter. Perhaps we can avoid another 5-month winter, which is frequently the norm for North Dakota.

Reflecting over the months, we have much to be grateful for this year. Not sure where to begin. Little Leo arriving in March was a fabulous gift to us. We wish we were closer to Berkeley, of course. Becoming grandparents is AWESOME! There is a good reason why this kind of parenting is considered *grand*.

Every day of my cancer journey has been eventfully eye-opening. I find myself looking retrospectively at the past six months. I am keenly aware of the superb medical care, and the love & concern expressed by friends and family. Seriously, I am grateful for breast cancer. I have seen the best in people.

MY STORY

January 10

Ok, you sneaky someone...thank you for your kindness. I love the pulchritudinous Mary, Joseph and Baby Jesus carved statue left between our doors on Saturday night. And for a bonus, you left a bag of Milano double chocolate cookies. THANK YOU!! The card simply said:

A gift for little Christmas—Even the Wise Men had their "off" days!

And, how do you like that robust adjective? Purdy audacious, don't you think? Incidentally, pulchritudinous means beautiful. My dad would be so proud of me for using a big word. He loved them—the bigger/the better.

Theresa, my asthmatic friend, ran a half marathon in Florida (Disney World) this past weekend. I am so proud of her. She has the loveliest smile! Bet she was BEAMING as she crossed the finish line. She also is AWESOME ALICE to me as she cleans our home every other week (thanks to Pete and Mary for hiring her to do so!). I don't know who to thank first. How's that for a useful gift?

Unexpected gifts. Isn't life extra special when unexpected, kind things take place? One blessing following another.

January 12

This week I had a new professional head shot taken. Oh my goodness—do I look like my mother, Audrey! I catch my reflection from time to time and find myself remarking, *what happened to Kim?* The grey hair is going to take some getting used to—but it is hair, nonetheless!! Kindly rejoice with me.

The woman behind the counter at the photo studio asked what kind of cancer I had. When I told her, "Breast," she smiled sweetly and told me she had a friend that had breast cancer whose hair, being black all her life, grew back in a shade of strawberry blonde. I asked her what color her friend's hair was today. She became rather quiet and then said, "She died. It never went back to black."

Back to the clinical trial, the study is looking at whether Metformin, an agent commonly used to treat diabetes, can decrease or affect the ability of breast cancer cells to grow and whether Metformin will work with other therapy to keep cancer from recurring.

It is a randomized study meaning I'll either be on the medication or on a placebo. Both Dave and I agree that if this is something that can expedite a cure, or help me (and other breast cancer survivors) live longer without a recurrent cancer—it's all good.

Fargo has turned cold. After days of record highs, tonight it is bitter (7 above). I came home from radiation and took a hot bubble bath. Guess what? My conclusion...life is so very good.

> *Not everyone possesses a conspicuous talent. We are not equally blessed with great intellect or physical beauty or emotional strength. But we all have been given the same ability to be faithful.*
>
> Gigi Tchividjian Graham

I intend to remain faithful, dear one. Keep warm. Sleep tight.

where do you find your strength?

I can do all things through Christ
who gives me strength.

Philippians 4:13

I experienced excruciating pain during childbirth. In the throes of transitioning from stage one to stage two ("Really, you're suggesting it will hurt more than *this?*") to stage three ("No pushing until the doctor arrives"), I thought there could be no pain worse.

Yes, it was difficult and I could not have done it without an encouraging husband, an experienced

Family Friends Faith

doctor, and numerous competent nurses. At the conclusion, a cone-headed baby resembling a hairy monkey was placed in my arms, and the agonizing pain associated with labor and delivery? *Poof!* All gone. My point? After insufferable pain, an odd, breathing entity with a portion of my genetic make-up was given to me to take home, to love and adore for a few years, and then, with minimal instructions, to send it (him, and later, her, and him, and him) out into the world on its own. It's important to remember: "This too shall pass." Pain, sorrow, grief, heartache—all shall pass. And we will be more resilient in the aftermath.

I asked random people where they find their strength. Here are some of their answers:

In classical music

In inspirational movies that make me cry

In steroids (really!)

From my family

By believing that God is in control

By doing something nice for someone else

Rejuvenating with a good night's sleep

My strength is found in weakness

In determination to never, ever quit; carry on

By knowing that God is with me every step of every day

For me, I find strength in the three "F's": family, friends, and faith. When diagnosed with stage three breast cancer, I could not go it alone. And

I didn't have to. My family was ever-present. My friends were steadfast and true. And the faith community I am a part of surrounded me with tender loving care.

Cancer sharpened my focus on the important things in life. Replacing the basement carpeting and redoing the rock garden in the backyard were no longer at the top of my to-do list.

I've heard it said that going through cancer uncovers a huge discovery. I'd like to suggest that going through cancer is a gift to the participant. Every day is fresh and new, and as a cancer survivor, I want to make every day count for something. I have witnessed first-hand that the key to a joyful life is frequently *missed* by millions of *healthy* people. Prior to cancer, why would I ever have considered spending an afternoon watching a robin build a nest or taking in the aroma of burning leaves in the fall? Listening to a baby's cry, watching a child learn to ride a bike, counting the colored stripes on a rainbow, hanging clothes outdoors on a clothesline just to experience the *smell* of clean sheets—

seriously, are such everyday, mundane simplicities worthy of one's attention?

Odd. What is worthy of one's attention? Goodness, I was born with nipples and thought I would die with nipples. Isn't that important stuff? Isn't life full of changes?

> I can do **all things** through **Christ** who gives me strength.
> Philippians 4:13

I would not want to live now as I did prior to breast cancer. Something in me has changed—for the better. Where do I find my strength? By simply believing that everything happens for a reason and brings personal growth in due season. More than anything, I believe that "I can do all things through Christ who gives me strength."

January 21

I've been told that, *this life is a dress rehearsal.*

Years ago, I thrived in the theatre. There was always an audition process. Then callbacks. Then a cast list would get posted and either my name made the list, or did not. In the best case scenario, I would get cast in a leading role and the work began in earnest. Eventually, after weeks of study, it would be the night of dress rehearsal. By this time, it was imperative that all lines and blocking were committed to memory. No mistakes. Frequently I would dream about the current show—quite sure I would speak lines in my sleep. It was critically important to have everything in place and have a favorable dress rehearsal to ensure the success of the show. I needed to be *ready.*

Makes me think—I want to be ready for heaven. Today is a dress rehearsal. I want to be ready. Breast cancer has made me look at each day as a sweet, undeserved gift. To say *I appreciate today* would be an understatement. It's a gift, a dress rehearsal—a time to prepare and have everything in place.

I hope I have 20 years (or more!) to partici-pate in the dress rehearsal. However—if my days are limited and I manage to forget my lines en route to heaven, I'm hopeful that I won't be dismissed from the cast party. It's going to be the *best* party ever.

January 22

Little Leo

I spent an hour Skyping with Leo tonight. He lives in California. I just love him to bits. Jesus, in your free time, kindly wrap him in your tender arms and let him know how precious he is to you.

I want my kids and grandkids to look to you, Lord, to fulfill their longings. This world can't begin to give them the contentment which you offer.

Leo is a hoot and handful. Incidentally, he got kicked out of daycare for biting. Such a perfect little man.

February 26

All is very good, from my limited perspective. I feel stronger each week and dismiss my on-going fatigue as residual effects from various treatments. A cancer survivor mentioned that she felt exhausted for several months following treatment. She remarked that the one year anniversary from her diagnosis was her turning point. If that be the case, by mid-June, I will be up and running full speed again.

Life just continues on, right? Our son, Isaac's wedding is less than two months away, April 14. It will be delightful to have so many of our immediate and extended family/friends together in one location.

Dave notes, my once golden locks are now dark with silver tips, amounting to 2 1/2 inches. I am, indeed (Dave loves to use the word, INDEED), something to behold.

Also, RIP to Gene Miller of Crookston, MN. My favorite "horse wrangler" of all time. My guess is that he and my father, Randy are working on a covered wagon for their next trail ride. Sawdust on the heavenly floorboards—can't you just smell it?

MY STORY

March 1

Mary's mama, Ursula, went home to Jesus yesterday. My heart is so sad for Mary and her dad, Don, and her brothers...but certainly not for Ursula.

While in the middle of chemo this past summer, Mary delivered a "Prayer Plant" from her parents, explaining the significance of its curling leaves in the evening. So often Mary would tell me that she had spoken with her mom and reported that Ursula had been praying for my recovery and healing.

My hope is that my mom, Audrey was on the welcoming committee and gave Ursula a hearty welcome, introducing her to the altos in the heavenly chorus.

I've heard rumors that Ursula was a marvelous organist in her day and taught her daughter all kinds of sweet songs as she grew up. Just unclear if she was a serious singer. Mary has the loveliest alto voice I've heard—so I'm making an assumption that Ursula will be invited to stand by my mom for choir practice. They will be singing praises, I have no doubts.

R.I.P. Ursula. I promise to take good care of your little girl.

March 24

Frequently people ask me if I am cured—or in remission. Is there an answer? How does one know for sure? Anyone who has dealt with cancer will never be the same and the answer to that "cured" question is a crazy unknown.

What's going on in your heart, friend? I am soon crawling into bed and saying my prayers for the evening. I am remembering you and how sweet your presence is in my life. Whether we have been friends for years or you just know me as your pastor's wife, or possibly as the lady that had (past tense!) breast cancer—I am grateful for YOU. Rest tonight knowing that you are loved.

what's your battle wound?

Recently, I spoke at a large church in southern Minnesota. The audience was engaged. They laughed, wiped tears, smiled at one another, and nodded periodically—all at appropriate times. When I asked rhetorical questions, some offered answers. And no one was sleeping! —I seriously love this kind of group!

For this particular presentation, I noted that, as women, we all have one or more battle wounds, and yet, due in large part to women's feisty nature, we are astonishingly resilient. I hoped to impart the message that we all deal with wounds, not

The most beautiful people we have known are those who have known defeat, known suffering, known struggle, known loss, and have found their way out of the depths. These persons have an appreciation, a sensitivity, and an understanding of life that fills them with compassion, gentleness, and a deep loving concern. Beautiful people do not just happen.

Elizabeth Kubler-Ross

just those that are stitched up, but some which are deeply buried—many, we hope, will never be obvious, never displayed. I noted that we, as women, are very good at camouflaging heartache. I listed a few of these *hidden* wounds: a deteriorated, loveless marriage; unresolved family dysfunction; financial concerns; addictions to porn or gambling; ongoing attempts at "keeping up with the Joneses"—and failing. And failing. And failing. I asserted that it is considerably easier to deal with external wounds, such as, in my case, healing from a bilateral mastectomy, than to deal with the many internal wounds that we want to believe no one else can see. We are resilient. "I am woman—hear me roar!"

At the conclusion, I received a standing ovation from over six hundred women. I was deeply humbled by their response. After several minutes of embracing and thanking attendees, I ended up at the back of the auditorium signing my books.

I noticed a young woman at the back of the line, encouraging others to step ahead of her. Several minutes later, the line was eliminated—the majority of attendees had left for home—and she stood before me. Just the two of us. Our eyes locked. She was model-striking with long, straight blonde hair and bold, turquoise eyes—genuinely gorgeous. I found myself thinking, *Perhaps in heaven I will look so good.*

"I am thirty-seven years old," she volunteered. "I have an awesome husband and two little girls."

"That's wonderful!" I replied. "I remember those years with little ones—your fun has just begun!"

Her eyes shifted, unable to maintain eye contact with me. I asked, "Do you want me to sign a book for you, Dear Heart?"

"No." she responded. "I am not ready to read about this quite yet." There was a lengthy pause before she said, "But I do have something to ask of you." She bit her lip and those exquisite eyes filled with tears. "I've been diagnosed with cancer, too. On Tuesday," she continued, "I'm scheduled for a bilateral mastectomy."

Shit. Another cancer sister. Breast cancer is not very discriminating. Young—this beauty queen was far too young, with far too much yet to experience.

Under normal circumstances, like my father, I am quick on my feet and able to converse with anyone about anything. However, all I could mutter was, "I am so sorry." It seemed so terribly inadequate. "How can I help you?"

Again, a long, awkward pause. "Okay. I'll just ask," she smiled self-consciously. "Will you show me your scars?" Then she blurted, "Oh, for God's sake. This is so silly and I am sorry. Wow—so embarrassing—I don't know what made me think to ask you such a personal thing. Forgive me." She abruptly turned to leave.

Now it made sense. Waiting till everyone was gone. Not knowing how to ask. "No, wait," I said. She turned back to my table. "Of course you can see my scars. They aren't pretty, but they are *my* battle wounds. I'm actually quite proud of them."

She smiled and wiped a tear from her face. Standing up, I moved to her and gave her a quick hug. "Thanks for asking. Let's find a restroom."

That's what transpired. We found a bathroom and actually got the giggles as I began my little strip-tease show for this sweet woman. Removing my top and sexy (not!) Amoena bra containing two prostheses, I told her, "You'll be surprised how heavy these babies can be—depending on the size you choose." And then I stood—buck naked from the waist up, scars on display. She was quiet, taking it all in.

I'm unsure how long this moment lasted, but finally she said, "You know, it's not so bad. I was expecting worse." She smiled—a radiant, confident smile. "I think I can do this."

"Of course you can! If I can do it, *you* can do it!" I quickly dressed, and we headed out the door.

She inquired, "By the way, do you plan on having reconstruction someday?"

"Doubtful," I answered. "At my age, I really don't *need* the girls anymore. No more babies planned—though my husband thinks we should keep trying!" I grinned. "Really, I think he is fine with me just like this—without the girls. Although he's due for an eye exam, he still thinks I'm beautiful. All good."

Before parting, I gave her a book, insisting that she take a peek at it when the time was right. Another quick embrace. I stuck my business card in her hand and told her she could call me anytime, and I promised to pray for her on Tuesday. She gave me a squeeze and sighed, "You *do* know that you are beautiful, don't you?"

In the craziness that morning, I neglected to ask her name and, sadly, never heard back from her to learn the outcome of her surgery. However, I think of her from time to time—this young, vivacious mother and wife who, like me, was thrown into a life interruption called breast cancer.

MY STORY

April 17

It's official. We celebrated the marriage of our eldest son, Isaac and his beautiful bride, Melissa this past Saturday, April 14 in Lincoln, Nebraska. They are a stunning pair and we met many of Melissa's family—all just as sweet as she is (great genetic pool).

Wedding day weather? Could not be worse. The national news named Lincoln the HOT SPOT for bad weather over the weekend. And, that certainly proved to be the case. We experienced severe thunder storms and tornado activity. A major Husker football game ended up being cancelled on Saturday afternoon; obviously serious weather considerations.

But, the wedding went on. Melissa looked like a Greek Goddess in her stunning dress. And, Isaac proved to be a handsome groom—I am, of course, partial. They make a darling couple. Prior to Saturday, I had never witnessed them kissing. It was lovely to see how much they care for each other.

I hope their married life is full of laughter, love and just a few challenges—to make the ride adventuresome and grace filled.

I have a PET scan scheduled next week to see if any cancer can be seen. One day at a time.

May 2

Our congregation is hosting its annual "Cabaret"—a night of fun and music—this coming Saturday. Dave and I will be singing, though unsure what the song will be. It is a joy to sing with my husband. We used to sing a LOT together—then life got busy and we had excuses. We are humbled and thankful as this year's free-will offering is going to help with my medical expenses. How kind is that?

May 4

*Suffering is more or less inevitable in
life, but it's not redemptive unless we
allow God to make good use of it.*
Molly Wolf

My PET scan report came back clear. From
the report it states: NO EVIDENCE OF RE-
CURRENT OR METASTATIC DISEASE. This is
the best possible news one can hear.

I have sincerely attempted to allow God to
use me and make the very best of this situation with my breast cancer. And, when I've
been patient, he has shared more grace with
me than I ever deserved.

So, rejoice with me over good report from PET
scan and rejoice that we have a Savior who
loves us all—even those of us with no breasts.

June 4

One year ago, I had no idea I had breast cancer.

That isn't exactly the truth, but nothing had been officially diagnosed yet. I had a *sense* something was wrong—just unsure *what* exactly. Isn't it wacky how much can change in a matter of days?

Nothing earth shattering has happened recently. Mostly simple, on-going events that continue to make up chapters in the journey.

I spoke at an event last week for the American Cancer Society and conversed with a woman who had breast cancer about five years ago. She reminded me that it takes a GOOD two years after surgery and treatment before energy and stamina return to normal. Seriously, I keep thinking I should be able to keep the schedule I had before I got sick. What does this thing called *patience* look like?

My word today is GRATEFUL. I am giddy with gratefulness to you for taking the time to think of me (& read my journal entries). AND, to God who turns caterpillars into butterflies. Can't wait to see what color he is painting my wings!

June 5

Article in the Fargo FORUM

Two Fargo pastors deal with diagnosis of cancer in women they love

By: Sherri Richards, INFORUM

FARGO - For the past year, the Revs. David Wagner and Chris Waldvogel have been on parallel paths.

Not just because both are pastors of Beautiful Savior Lutheran Church in south Fargo. Both dealt with a diagnosis of cancer in women they love.

Wagner's wife, Kim, had breast cancer while Waldvogel's mother, Suzanne, faced pancreatic cancer.

As pastors, their role is to walk with church members through hard times. Suddenly both of the 750-member congregation's ministers faced their own difficult journeys at the same time.

"It was an opportunity for the people here to uphold me," David says.

A similar journey
The timeline for each family's battle was eerily similar, the pastors acknowledge, though hundreds of miles separated the patients.

Kim, of Fargo, was diagnosed with breast cancer after a biopsy in early June last year.

Suzanne, who lives near St. Louis, was told she had pancreatic cancer in mid-June after a bout of jaundice caused by a blocked bile duct.

Both were Stage 3. Both women had surgery. Kim had a double mastectomy July 1. Days later, Suzanne underwent a Whipple procedure in which her gallbladder, duodenum and parts of the pancreas, intestines and stomach were removed.

Both endured rounds of chemotherapy and radiation. And last month, both were told they were cancer-free, though neither woman fully embraces that declaration.

Throughout their battles, the congregation expressed concern for both their pastors with kind words, regular inquiries and prayer.

"The whole community here enveloped us with prayer," Kim says. "I have never seen compassion expressed as it was after being diagnosed. It was overwhelming. There was never a day I didn't feel prayerfully uplifted."

Caring cards

The congregation organized a card shower. Members sent greeting cards to both Kim and Suzanne, with the goal of each woman receiving a card a day.

In the end, they received regular mail for more than three months.

Church member Mardi Schlichtmann says the effort was a quiet way for the congregation to show its support and uplift the two women.

"People want to help, but sometimes you don't know what to do or what to say," she says.

Members were encouraged to send funny or thoughtful cards, kid drawings or handwritten messages.

Suzanne says throughout her diagnosis and treatment she felt at peace and kept her emotions in check, until she started getting the cards from the folks in Fargo.

"A lot of them wrote these lovely notes along with the cards, and it totally overwhelmed me. These were people I didn't know," she says, choking up with tears again.

"I see how much that support has meant to me and my mother," Chris says, "just given her assurance that there's something bigger than her disease at work."

Because the Wagners were in Fargo, members brought food and flowers, helped tidy the house, and accompanied Kim on chemo appointments, David and Kim say.

Beautiful Savior's praise band donated proceeds from its annual cabaret show, held May 5, to the Wagners to help cover extra expenses.

Effect on ministry

David says while he knows medical crises happen all the time, going through one made it more real and opened his eyes.

"I think it will strengthen both of their ministries," Kim says.

So many congregants will face breast cancer or other challenges, she says. Looking at her husband, she adds, "You'll have a respect for what they're going to be going through."

Suzanne says she knows both pastors had extra responsibilities because of what each was going through. "I know Chris had some bad days; I know he was so worried," Suzanne says.

"In many ways I did struggle with a bit of guilt for not being there," Chris says.

Suzanne told him he could pray for her from Fargo just as well as he could have in St. Louis.

She also sees a silver lining to their coinciding journeys.

"I felt bad that they had to go through that both at the same time, and yet the other thought that occurred to me was, it was maybe a lesson to everyone to know that bad things do happen to good people, and God never promises us that we won't have bad things happen. But he does promise he'll be there with us," Suzanne says.

Suzanne Waldvogel lost her battle
with cancer on
February 19, 2013
Rest in Peace.

June 12

Joy again!

A year has passed since all this began. 12 months! I'm still here.

Must tell you about a wonderful experience today. I was asked to speak for the LIFE AFTER BREAST CANCER *Taking Care of You* Seminar at the Holiday Inn.

It brought me more joy than I can explain. Sheer joy. This event is really done up right and the attendees are all so appreciative. The vendors were gracious—beautiful things for sale. Lovely.

One year ago I attended this same event (different speakers/topics) and was so freshly diagnosed that I spent most of the day wiping tears away. Today was different!

I've been through many difficult days—and feel now like a veteran warrior. Survived stage 3 breast cancer! Woohoo! Surgeries, 16 chemo treatments, 33 radiation treatments—I made it through.

I visited with dozens of women—we all have much in common. One woman has had five re-occurrences of her initial breast cancer. The last came back in her brain. How dare I complain? The last thing she shared with me, "There is always someone worse off than me." What an amazing woman!

I shared with the group that 24 hours before I had my bilateral mastectomy I had profession-al pictures taken—many showing my breasts. Even though I will never profess to be a "pin-up" model, these "girls" were much appreci-ated. They nourished four babies and every child developed a sincere fondness for their soft comfort when a boo-boo needed loving.

Knowing my breasts would soon be labeled as specimen #1 and #2 (I pictured them in lab dishes), I wanted true to life pictures of them. The photographer that agreed to do this for me, is an ARTIST. I will forever be grateful that she said yes—to something she had never considered doing before. Thank you, Meg! You are so awesome—your work is astounding.

I mentioned that my life is richer due to cancer partnering with me on the journey. I continue to believe this with my whole heart.

I took Reggie for a long walk tonight. It is about 70 degrees out everything is so green and fresh, following the rainfall on Sunday. He loves to be out with me and the evening is PERFECT.

All is so very good in my world right now. I hope you can say the same. Have I told you that you are a sweet treasure in my life?

August 18

I am having a hysterectomy on August 30. I was advised to have my ovaries removed— and will get that taken care of Thursday morning. It will be nice to have it done. My doctor/surgeon, Jon Dangerfield (that is his REAL name!) is outstanding.

My sister, Pat is coming to stay with me to keep me from "overdoing". My plan is to feel good enough to play cards and read some books I've set aside—for a time such as this.

We will let you know how everything turns out. Unsure as to how long I'll be out of commission, but I don't sit still very well. So, I hope to mend quickly and back to work ASAP.

September 2

No pain pills today. Surgery was a breeze.

I have very little pain. In fact, on the hospital pain scale of 1 - 10, I presently rate my pain at 0. Occasionally my lower back aches, comparable to that of early labor—but it passes.

I feel good enough to go for a walk with my dogs tonight—BUT, my constant companion, Pat is telling me NOOOOOOOOO. And, she is right, but—I still feel good enough to do so.

September 11

I am having my Celsite Implantable Access Venous Port System removed tomorrow. I've had it since July 20, 2011 and it's time for it to come out. Good news—they must feel I'm cancer free at present, or close to it. It feels like I'm saying goodbye to a good friend as it's been with me through a lot of chemo treatments, blood draws and flushes this past year.

Initially, I detested this thing. I told Dave that it felt like I had periodical bee bites occurring. He would roll his eyes. Then, when discussing discomforts with my oncologist, I was told that others also mentioned the same sensation of BEE bites. See, I am not crazy!

Once that passed, the port was incredibly convenient. I loved the ease of having it accessed for chemo treatments & blood draws.

Thus, I am bound and determined to take this little gadget home with me tomorrow. How much do you want to bet the medical community won't let me? Not including the fee for the doctor to install it, I paid $1800 for this device. By golly, don't you think I should be able to have it, now that it's coming out? They certainly don't have further use of it (or do they recycle these handy ports?). It's mine, I tell you! I will forever love *show and tell* items. This is a dandy and I want it.

Speaking of show and tell, when I had my hysterectomy on August 30, I asked Dr. Dangerfield if I might have my uterus and ovaries to take home with me. My kind surgeon rolled his eyes at me and said, "Goodnight, Kim." That's the last thing I recall before waking up in recovery. Darn it. No one takes me very seriously.

Please watch for further updates. There may be harsh words expressed if I am told *nay* regarding the port.

September 12

My trip to Interventional Radiology this morning was stellar.

The answer? NO

OK. If I had a blood-borne disease, I can understand why I couldn't take home my used port. However, I am quite healthy excepting my past year with breast cancer.

My doctor informed me that due to health regulations, I could not have the port that was originally inserted into my chest wall. I attempted the temper tantrum routine and the, "But I've paid for it!" jargon. In the end, the doctor provided me with the same kind of port and tubing that had been used, but was actually NEW, in its sterile wrapping. I must look rather impish as he informed me that I should not attempt to sell it on Craig's List. Golly...*that* was right at the top of my THINGS TO DO list.

I was also given a nifty picture of the port in my chest before removal and then a picture of my chest following removal.

My port is gone and there's a big bandage in its place. In 48 hours I can remove the bandage and of course, *ooh and ahhh* over my new little battle wound. Show & Tell is going to be the highlight of my week.

September 28

I spoke for the Sanford Hospital Embrace program's 4th annual cancer survivorship picnic last night at the Bluestem Center for Arts. It was fabulous!

There were over 500 people in attendance—and proved to be an evening I won't soon forget.

The picnic was for cancer survivors and their support system. I saw many familiar faces—and met many new friends! I felt privileged & honored (& seriously humbled) to be asked to share my story.

While sharing, I mentioned that I found the statement issued by President Obama following the July Aurora, Colorado tragedy very apropos to anyone dealing with cancer. He commented:

> *"If there is anything to take away from this tragedy (our cancer journey – Kim's add), it's a reminder that life is fragile. Our time here is limited and it is precious. And what matters in the end are not the small and trivial things, which often consume our lives. It's how we choose to treat one another and love one another. It's what we do on a daily basis to give our lives meaning and to give our lives purpose. That's what matters. That's why we're here."*

My advice: Forget the small and trivial things. Stay cozy-close to those you love.

October 10

I celebrated my 52nd birthday yesterday. It was a perfect day.

Thanks to everyone who jotted a note on FACEBOOK extending birthday greetings and for the cards and flowers. You know who you are—thank you for your kindness. Even a cupcake I received; the prettiest and yummiest I've tasted. Such fun!

My surgeon told me to work at home until Oct. 15. So, as of Monday, I will have no restrictions and can gallop about at full force. Can't wait!

So much to do in this year ahead. Watch out world—here I come.

MY STORY

I am feeling great! 16+ months since my diagnosis. I'm surviving, actually flourishing quite nicely.

Once again, I am thinking about life and how unsettling it is—often not making much sense. Pretty random. We are born, we cry a bit, laugh a bit, and touch a life here and there while having others touch ours, and suddenly we are found in a great cloud of witnesses that have gone on before us. Won't heaven be interesting/exciting?

I have an appointment with my oncologist tomorrow morning. I believe I am scheduled to see her every four months for the first couple of years following my cancer diagnosis. I am feeling good, pleased to report. Though these rainy, dreary days make me tired. You too? Lately I have been tempted to crawl into my bed, cover up with my down comforter and read away the day!

I hope you are joyful and exuding gladness in all you do today and in your days ahead. I encourage you to love deeply and without regrets.

April 20

My sweet friend Pamela made it into heaven in the wee hours of the morning I saw her earlier this week. She was so ready to pack up and be on her way. But, she stuck around much longer than anyone expected. Although she responded only through her eyes, I told her to get ready to catch the next flight out, reminding her that her daughters and husband would be ok, her dog, Santi would be loved and she didn't need to stick around for any of us.

The last time I spoke with her was a few weeks back when she still could communicate. I asked her what remained on her bucket list. She grinned and said, she only longed to see a warm spring day. Well, we still have snow here in ND—but the sun is shining today. I am so glad to know Pam is enjoying the warmth of heaven. It's got to be even better than a warm spring day! Pam thanked me many times over for "saving her life" on Dec. 19 when a thinned artery (due to radiation/chemo for esophageal cancer) in her neck burst while she was at work and I happened to be the first on the scene to apply pressure to her carotid so she wouldn't bleed to death. Pam later informed me that she had no tunnel experiences with great bursts of light on the end. "No *come to Jesus* experience, Kim" she told me.

So, Pam was given a few more months to love and to be loved. I will miss her and our conversations about the unfairness of cancer, the worth of true friends, and the things in life that actually are meaningful.

RIP dear one. Just like breast cancer, you too changed my life for the better.

I feel so good. I cherish the speaking opportunities I've had recently and my marketing efforts are paying dividends. I see little glimmers of grace every day.

Today I read a great piece by Joel Osteen that speaks to my heart:

> *Today, I want to remind you of what God says about you. No matter what's happening in your life today, remember: you are not limited by your resources, your family or your background. Almighty God has equipped and empowered you. He has given you creativity, ideas, inventions, skills and talents. Don't you dare settle for a mediocre life! Today, I call forth the seeds of greatness inside of you. Today, I declare that your best days are ahead.*

I can't wait to see what lies ahead for me.

bff's

I love my girlfriends. They have helped me get through some of my most challenging seasons in life. The common terminology nowadays is "best friend forever," or BFF (plural: best friends forever; BFFs).

Have I mentioned that I birthed four children in six years? Over the years, I have come to believe that an embellished tiara—one with diamonds and pearls—awaits me at the heavenly gates. Despite what others may say, I earned this crown—really.

It's absolutely the truth: If not for Nan, Sally, and Midge, my BFFs at different times, I'm not sure I would have made it when the kids were small. Perhaps better stated, I don't know if the *kids* would have made it.

While Dave attended seminary in St. Louis, a few seminarian wives connected and started a child exchange program. I would take Nan's children once a week, and then she'd take mine for another day. It was marvelous to have a break from the pandemonium and unruliness of our home—if just for a day. This day off each week saved me, saved our marriage, and saved our children from being sold to the highest bidder.

Friends are like bras, close to your **heart** and all about **support.**

As part of his study in the ministry, Dave was assigned to a field-work congregation, St. Jacobi, in a St. Louis suburb. Its membership was composed primarily of faithful, beautiful, loud-singing African American families.

Every Sunday morning, Sally, a large-bosomed black woman, met me at the church entrance (sometimes even at our car as we unloaded the kids) with outstretched arms. In a splendid deep southern drawl, she commanded, "Give me yo babies!" She couldn't wait to get Isaac and Margot tucked into her ample arms. I would surrender my two tots—born eleven months apart—to be re-united with them a full three hours later. I have no idea how Sally entertained them each Sunday morning as she disappeared with diaper bag and two babies in tow. All I knew for sure was that Sally's act of kindness was a source of weekly deliverance for me.

Our third child, Lucas, was born at the Missouri Baptist Hospital in St. Louis, one week prior to

Dave taking his final exams at seminary. In 1987, he accepted his first call in the ministry. We loaded up our station wagon with three children and headed to western North Dakota, where Dave served the dual parishes of St. Paul's Lutheran Church in Beach and St. Peter's Lutheran Church in Belfield.

During those years of living in Beach, Midge was my BFF. She was a member of our small church, where we sang duets, created liturgical banners, and attended Lutheran Women's Missionary League (LWML) functions. It became clear to me while living there, that in small towns, church affiliation was of great importance. Midge and I adhered to this, dutifully.

In hopes of getting physically fit, we walked the streets of town, confiding and commiserating. This is what girlfriends do.

Our youngest child, Abram was born in Glendive, Montana in 1988. In a May thunderstorm, we hauled our newborn son home to the parsonage

behind the church, swelling the population of Beach to 1,079. The church threw us a potluck dinner in his honor. That's the kindness this rural town offered to their pastor's family.

When I was exhausted, Midge would take my four children for a few hours, allowing me time to recharge from parsonage/church/family responsibilities and bedlam. During the years we lived there, I was a recipient of her ongoing generosity and friendship. What would my life in Beach, North Dakota, have been without Midge?

Years ago, while discussing this observation with my mother, she astutely said, "Kim, God always supplies a Midge when you need one." My mom was the smart one in her family.

I once heard actress and breast cancer survivor Jaclyn Smith share with CNN, "One of the most important things you can do is remember the power of girlfriends . . . Girlfriends saved my day."

I agree. There is enormous power in girlfriends.

Presently, I have a couple girlfriends whom I count as BFFs. At least they are my BFFs for this particular season of my life. Frequently, over dinner or as we drive a distance to our next "gig," we share fragmented bits and pieces of our days. Our conversations are filled with life's chronicles: Weight loss, weight gain. Favorite clothing trends and where to find the best deals. Topics range from the mundane to the controversial. Some joyful and others causing us to wipe tears and offer hugs. We talk about children, grandchildren, dreams, and disappointments, all the while applauding each other's accomplishments. We have an unspoken motto: What is spoken here, stays here. We haven't resorted to swearing on a Bible, but the premise is the same.

When my cancer diagnosis was announced, of course I turned to my husband and immediate family for support. Then, I turned to my girlfriends—my BFFs.

And they have been with me through it all. Oh, there is power in girlfriends!

My two BFFs and I have created a comedy routine, and have been asked—actually paid!—to perform at numerous events over the past years. Calling ourselves "The Luscious Grape Suzettes," we dress in attractive purple evening gowns and serenade audiences with songs such as "The Rose" and "Stop in the Name of Love." With tight three-part harmony, we sing and dance (choreography is questionable). And then, the grand finale. We return to the stage dressed in ABBA-style spandex attire and ratted hairdos. Saving the best for last, we sing "Dancing Queen" and "Super Trouper." At least we would like to think it is our *best*.

Seriously, how many girlfriends would be willing to do this?

I love my girlfriends—my BFFs for each given season of life. Thank you for sharing your incredible lives with me.

My Dearest Kim,

You made it—two years and counting.

Today marks the second anniversary of your surgery. I am so glad that you are still here with me. You are a joy. You are a very beautiful, talented, and caring person. I am the luckiest man to have you as my wife, friend, and companion. I hope we have many, many more years together.

I will love you always!

Dave

ACKNOWLEDGEMENTS

My sincere thanks to the many people who have made a lasting imprint on my journey with breast cancer.

I experienced exceptional care from: Timothy Mahoney, MD; Mark Gitau, MD; Michael Bouton, MD; Dennis Bier, MD; and Shelby Tierstrip, MD. The nurses and technicians working in Oncology and Radiology are outstanding.

Annette Wood, graphic designer/creative genius—you are so much fun to work with! Heidi Mann, editor—you are an exceptional wordsmith. My book took on it's own *life* under your guidance.

To my husband Dave, four beautiful children, and three grandsons who give me reason to **celebrate** every single day.

My thanks to God, who has carried me throughout this entire journey.

Pictures

CPSIA information can be obtained at www.ICGtesting.com
Printed in the USA
LVOW01s1421300415

436285LV00006B/7/P